Cooking With The Ancients

Cooking With The Ancients

The Bible Food Book

Arlene Stadd

Glenbridge Publishing Ltd.

Illustrations
Patricia Hobbs

Library of Congress Catalog Card Number: LC 96-78375

International Standard Book Number: 0-944435-43-2

Printed in the U. S. A.

TO

My Mother

CONTENTS

INTRODUCTION

And the Lord God planted a garden eastward in Eden; and there he put the man whom he had formed. And out of the ground made the Lord God to grow every tree that is pleasant to the sight, and good for food; the tree of life also in the midst of the garden, and the tree of knowledge of good and evil.

(Genesis 2:8-9)

We can cook with the ancients, eat like them, but is there any reason why we should?

For over two thousand years, we've looked to the Bible for wisdom, solace, and spiritual support. No question, the Patriarchs knew a thing or two. The Book they left us is poetry, history, religious instruction — could it be a guide to physical sustenance as well?

The Good Book is direct. It documents the lives of people, *real* people. When the three strangers appear before Abraham and promise that his elderly wife, Sarah, shall finally have a son:

And Sarah heard it in the tent door, which was behind him. Now Abraham and Sarah were old and well stricken in age, and it ceased to be with Sarah after the manner of women. Therefore, Sarah laughed within herself, saying, After I am waxed old shall I have pleasure, my lord being old also? And the Lord said unto Abraham, wherefore did Sarah laugh, saying shall I of a surety bear a child, which am old? Is anything too hard for the Lord?

(Genesis 18:10-14)

According to Genesis, Sarah was 127. Can't you just see Sarah's knowing look and hear her laugh at the absurdity of becoming pregnant at her age?

Speaking of chronological age, the Bible lists some pretty remarkable ones: Jacob, 147 (described as an old father at 130); Joseph, 110; Aaron, 123 — as well as more usual spans: Jehoshaphat, 60; Azariah, 68; and Manasseh, 67.

Actually, a wide range of old age is seen. Isaac at 180 is described as old and contented with days, while King David at 70 is called old and stricken in years.

Aside from those extraordinary oldsters, in Psalms 90:10 we are told that our lifetime will last seventy years, and if we're lucky, eighty. "The days of our years are threescore years and ten; and if by reason of strength they be fourscore years, yet is their strength labour and sorrow; for it is soon cut off, and we fly away."

The fact that they announced threescore years and ten as the average length of a life would indicate that they were remarkably long-lived, taking into account the high rate of infant mortality, accidents and going off to war.

Even giving them that, why should we limit ourselves to the few choices available to Bible people? We have a diversity of foodstuffs today, a variety perhaps unparalleled in human history. Why look back?

Obviously, we're way beyond clay ovens. We have state-of-the-art ranges, radar, and convection ovens that do everything but spin straw into gold, micro-ovens that zap seven course dinners out of freeze-dried packets. No, there's no *necessity* for eating the way our forefathers ate.

But before we consider whether we should or should not, let's examine these ancestors of ours. Who exactly were they? What part of the world are we talking about?

The Biblical lands included the areas on both sides of the Jordan, Assyria in the north and Egypt in the southwest; spreading westward to the Mediterranean or Great Sea; south and east of the Dead Sea beyond the desert to the region between the Tigris and the Euphrates. The inhabitants were small wandering tribes of herders in the process of a monumental leap forward. For the first time, they were about to settle down in one place and stay put.

Which led to the next stage, developing a pastoral society of small, self-sufficient farms in a time of slow travel and hard work. Only if they produced a surplus, could the community begin to support people engaged in other activities besides growing food and shepherding livestock. Craftsmen, builders, artists, musicians, priests, and scribes would emerge, and the Sumerian cities developed centers of civilized association. Trade and commerce increased, a pictograph writing, bookkeeping, and mathematics began.

The fertile crescent was an arcade connecting north and south and a bazaar of trade between Asia and Africa. Even a cursory glance at the ingredients obtainable in antiquity makes its astonishing point — the people had a varied assortment of foods. More than we usually give them credit for.

One of the things that distinguishes us from animals is that animals live in the eternal present. We say that we believe it's a good idea, but we pat ourselves on the back for what we've lately accomplished. Perhaps it's part of our need to believe we're making progress, an all too human delusion. We tend to think that by being the latest we're the smartest. Don't we have computers, electronic marvels, space blastoffs? And that's only now. By next year . . .

Granted, we humans have come a long way. But although primitive people may have lacked our technical expertise, they weren't stupid. In the first early agricultural village to be excavated, Jarmo, in northeastern Iraq, archeologists found a typical house of 6700 B.C. constructed of the same building material used today in the Near East. The hinges on the doors were stone sockets for round-ended posts strong enough to keep out intruders when the doors were barred. And speaking of intruders, ancient cities unearthed in Palestine had walls as much as thirty feet thick!

Their houses were designed around central courtyards, so cooking in that warm climate could be accomplished out-of-doors; their ovens were built with fire doors and flues enabling the oven temperature to be regulated.

We have continued to make improvements, certainly. It can be said we stood on their shoulders. That may have given us the elevated perspective to gaze forward, riveting our eyes on the future. At the same time, we can take a moment to look backward respectfully at what will never change: family, social relationships, the cycle of life — those values without beginning or end. We can look also at the homely things: where we lay our heads at night, how we clothe our bodies, the kind of food we eat and how we prepare it, how we face life and death, freedom and tyranny — just as our forefathers did. The Hebrews dwelled in Egypt for 400 years. After their escape from bondage in the fifteenth century B.C., they lived a sedentary and peaceful number of years in the village culture of Palestine, primarily in the hill country. There they kept small herds of sheep and goats and farmed their terraced plots of land with wooden plows. This was known as the Settlement period. During the Monarchy years, when David began his forty-year reign about 1000 B.C., they went from a loosely formed tribal league to an urban-based culture with Jerusalem as the capital. During this time, David united the land and people of Israel and created an empire extending far beyond its borders.

In 721 B.C. the Assyrians captured the Israelite city of Samaria after a three-year siege, and the Israelites who weren't captured or killed fled.

The Persians overthrew the Babylonian Empire in 539 B.C., allowing the captive Israelites to return home and re-establish Jerusalem. Then the Greeks defeated the Persians. The Romans conquered the Greeks. What did all those people consider worth fighting for besides their very lives?

> *For length of days, and long life, and peace, shall they add to thee.*
>
> (Proverbs 3:2)

And the lands they defended?

> *. . . a land of corn and wine, a land of bread and vine-yards, a land of oil olive and of honey, that ye may live, and not die . . . .*
>
> (II Kings 18:32)

> *. . . every man under his vine and under his fig tree, from Dan even to Beersheba, all the days of Solomon.*
>
> (I Kings 4:25)

A lot has changed since, but that much hasn't. Long life and *peace,* a tree to sit under, a comfortable bed and a full belly are just as vital today as they were in the time of the Patriarchs.

What did they look like, these ancients? They were Semites, the group that dominated Mesopotamia and Syro-Palestine. They were short, the men averaging about five feet tall, with shoulder-length black hair, flat noses, swarthy skin and beards. Women's long hair was bound with beaded ropes or fastened with combs of bone, gold, or silver. Both sexes oiled their skin and hair to protect it from the dry climate. They wore leather sandals. Men's woolen tunics were knee-length and tied around the waist. They also wore robes over their tunics. Women wore a similar tunic and robe with gold and silver jewelry.

Even if we don't individually resemble them, Our Fathers were just as interested in health, both physical:

For I will restore health unto thee . . .

(Jeremiah 30:17)

and holistic:

Beloved, I wish above all things that thou mayest prosper and be in health, even as thy soul prospereth.

(Third Epistle of John 1:2)

Considering the times, they were reasonably healthy. Along with their unsullied air and water, Bible people enjoyed food that was for the most part locally grown and unprocessed, the same food our ancestors ate from the time they ceased being hunter-gatherers and began living in tribes up to the beginning of the Industrial Revolution. And yes, they chose from an amazing array of unadulterated ingredients, locally grown and fresh, consumed in the sweet open air before anyone figured out how to profit from fast food, chemical improvements, or long shelf life.

And speaking of health, unless you live in a part of the country or a part of the world that has naturally pure water (is there such a place?) there is some evidence that drinking the chlorinated, chemicalized stuff not only tastes awful, but it's bad for us. A scientific study in 1992 linked chlorinated drinking water to bladder and colon cancer, prompting the EPA to re-evaluate their standards. Whether they got around to that or not, it's up to us to take those findings to heart. There's a great temptation to shell out hard-earned money for drinking water, but to economize by cooking with the liquid you wouldn't see fit to drink. Why? Whether it's soup or the water in which we cook beans, we still ingest it.

In case we assume that variety came in with the invention of the cathode-ray tube, Holy Land farmers harvested beans, lentils, peas, onions, leeks and garlic, turnips, carrots, celery, asparagus, beets, radishes, lettuce, cucumbers, fruits and nuts, olives, herbs and spices such as cumin, mint, basil, coriander, anise, thyme, bay, fennel, saffron, sage, mustard, and capers. They also had barley, millet, and, of course, wheat. But not corn. The

Bible mentions it, but scholars believe they meant the word as a generic term for grain. Maize was a New World crop.

Cherries, apricots, peaches, and plums came by way of Persia and Mesopotamia, now Iraq, and were soon locally cultivated. So their diet was high in fiber, minerals, and vitamins. The kind you chewed, not popped.

Bread was made from wheat flour, both unleavened and yeast risen — also sourdough bread from wheat flour alone or mixed with other grains. And what bread! It was the true faith — the staff of life. The Hebrew word *"lechem"* refers to food in general, but it also means bread. They ate it with butter or honey, sprinkling it with sea salt right out of the Dead Sea. Laborers dunked their bread in sour wine. They drank milk and turned it into cheese and yogurt.

The early books of the Bible, especially Leviticus, go into much detail about what is and is not acceptable as burnt offerings to God and how meat is slaughtered, handled, and prepared. The dietary laws of the Hebrews were strict as to which animals they were permitted to eat. We are told that Bible people used meat sparingly, as an accompaniment to vegetables and grains. It was generally treated as a condiment, shredded and mixed in a dish with grains, vegetables, and olive oil much the way Asian people utilize meat today. The exception was on religious feast days or meals honoring guests.

We also note that they ate everything on an animal except the squeal. They didn't waste a thing. They prepared the brains, kidneys, feet, and tongues of wild and domestic, newborn and suckling creatures — anything that crawled, crept, swam, or fluttered away from them, all the while adhering to strict injunctions, unusual for that time, to be hygienic and merciful, not to mention loving.

> *And Joab said to Amasa, Art thou in health, my brother?*
> *And Joab took Amasa by the beard with the right hand to*
> *kiss him.*
>
> (Samuel II 20:9)

Today we are still searching for fitness. An increasing number of health practitioners recommend a partial or total vegetarian diet. It's interesting that even in Biblical times, vegetarianism was not unknown.

The Book of Daniel relates how Daniel and his friends were taken to live at King Nebuchadnezzar's court for three years. Soon after they arrived, Daniel informed the King's steward that he and his three friends didn't eat meat.

Even in those days, that anyone would voluntarily shun meat was disturbing. The King prided himself on the luxury of his table and the steward was aware of this. He did his best to talk the young man into it, but Daniel was unswayable. No meat.

The steward was shocked. Maybe he got the job because his predecessor had his hand in the till and now he needed to appear scrupulously honest, but whatever the reason, the fellow was understandably frightened. He begged Daniel to swallow his principles along with the roast goat like everybody else. Be a good guy. Don't make trouble.

"Sorry," Daniel said, "no flesh food."

The steward panicked. He could lose a hand. Or worse. (In the Bible, the steward is identified as a eunuch.)

Daniel didn't want to see the man suffer. He had a solution. He advised the steward not to tell anyone. Who would know what these people ate?

But the steward worried that two weeks of not living high on the hog would prove their downfall. Daniel and his friends would be so weak that the entire court would have no trouble figuring out they weren't eating brisket and would be sure to tell the king the steward was holding out, maybe selling the uneaten rations on the black market.

"Tell you what," said Daniel, "you give us ten days of veggies and if we look pale or faint while jogging, we'll eat what you 'normal' folks eat. Otherwise, you stop hassling us. What do you say?"

What could he say? The steward agreed.

After ten days — and this part will come as no surprise to resolute vegetarians — Daniel and his merry men outran, outjumped, and out benchpressed the meat chompers. Not only that, their cheeks were pink, their eyes sparkled, and they multiplied fractions in their heads. Daniel went on to decipher the King's dreams and became one of his chief miracle workers. It's all right there in the Bible:

> *And in all matters of wisdom and understanding, that the king enquired of them, he found them ten times better than all the magicians and astrologers that were in all his realm. And Daniel continued even unto the first year of king Cyrus.*
>
> (Daniel 1:20-21)

Some scholars might argue that instead of being a staunch vegetarian, Daniel refused to eat food that wasn't kosher. That's possible. But we prefer to believe that the Bible encourages us to move toward the day when the wolf lies down with the lamb and we all live together in peace. In that glorious time:

> *They shall not hurt nor destroy in all my holy mountain . . .*
>
> (Isaiah 11:9)

Maybe with the present widespread concern about good health, we'll discover that God's holy mountain isn't such a stretch after all — it might only amount to a hill of beans.

In *Cooking With the Ancients* we will attempt to eat what the ancients ate. Within reason. We exclude dining on sparrows, pigeons, doves, flamingos' tongues, ostrich, cranes, or peacocks — all of which were consumed by the Romans, if we are to believe the recipes of Apicius, the Roman Epicurean and best known authority on the secrets of Roman cookery, who wrote *De Re Coquinaria* in the late fourth and early fifth century A.D. He described one feast that included a roasted whole wild boar stuffed with live thrushes.

Ordinary Bible cooks prepared beef, lamb, goat, and mutton as well as many varieties of poultry and fish. So in the interest of authenticity when dining with the ancients you may do likewise if thou chooseth. Our own preference is to eschew flesh food entirely and to select from the Biblical pantry only what we've come to believe will build optimum health. But that's our preference, it may not be yours.

To complete the meal, the ancients served fresh fruits and berries, grapes, sweet dates, figs, honey, and nuts either alone or made into cakes, custards with eggs and milk and/or yogurt.

As a diet, it must have worked. There's no word in the old language for bachelor. Marrying young in Biblical times, a man might be a father at eighteen, a grandpa at thirty-eight, and a great-granddad at fifty-seven! At seventy-five, the old man bounced his great-great-grandchildren on his knee:

> *It shall be health to thy navel, and marrow to thy bones.*
>
> (Proverbs 3:8)

Ancestral diets were based on fresh fruits and vegetables, whole grains and beans, and very little meat, the same diet that nourished human beings for centuries in most parts of the world — food that kept them hale in body and mind. Because, of course, what we put into our bodies has a direct effect on our health, and that affects our moods and the quality of our lives.

So we invite you to spend quality time with the ancients, cook with them, break bread, lift a glass to their health and ours. While we can certainly prosper without adhering to their exact diet, just following the general principles can only help, especially if we adopt the concept of simplification as a way of life.

That's the purpose of this book, to try to glean what we can from their experience and to see if we can eat as they did. Maybe not completely and certainly not forever, but we can enjoy it from time to time and for special occasions. To create a Bible Dinner for our family and guests, entertaining strictly from the Book.

Ultimately it is one more thread in the tapestry that we choose to examine, unraveling it from our earliest roots, finding continuity, tradition, folklore. It is basic, it feeds us. And it's fun.

For doesn't the Good Book say:

> *The thing that hath been, it is that which shall be; and that which is done is that which shall be done: and there is no new thing under the sun.*
>
> (Ecclesiastes I:9)

On the other hand, it's just possible that everything old is new again!

COOKING NOTES

While every effort has been made to keep these recipes authentic by limiting ingredients to foods used by Biblical cooks, it hardly seems necessary to add that the above should be taken with a grain of salt — sea salt, preferably. But not from the Dead Sea, unless, of course, it's in your neighborhood.

For the rest of us, salt means salt. Mix means mix. The fact that we have blenders, food processors, and electric mixers shouldn't count as mortal sins — merely blessings.

The idea is to cook with the ingredients that were available to the ancients, *not* to use their recipes. For one thing, we don't have them. Bible people hinted at what they ate, not how they prepared it. Athenaeus in the second century A.D., wrote *The Deipnosophists* (*The Banquet of the Learned*) in which he described the classic Greek culinary scene, but it was only the Roman Apicius who left actual recipes.

So we see nothing wrong with making mayonnaise in the blender. As long as we use olive oil, eggs, lemon juice, and salt. The foods were all available then. We *could* beat the mixture with a wooden spoon if we had that kind of time, but we might prefer a wire whisk or, better yet, a modern food processor. What counts is that mayonnaise was enjoyed during the Hellenistic period and possibly earlier.

Adapting their way of eating to ours is, therefore, easy and comfortable. We can modify modern recipes if we omit the obvious New World items and if we substitute honey for sugar and yeast for leavening ingredients such as baking powder and baking soda.

And speaking of ingredients, a note here about the eggs and butter and cream in many of these recipes. It's obvious that the ancients never were obsessed with reducing diets. It was all they could do to keep their bellies filled and their children fed. (Plenty of people today have the same problem.) They were more active than most of us moderns and that helped. But for those who are cutting down on rich food for whatever reason—health, fitness, or aesthetics—a grain of common sense goes down well with the Dead Sea salt. Occasional dinner parties are one thing, day after day feasting something else. If you're on a special low-fat diet, you'll still find plenty of ways to emulate our forebears without prematurely joining them.

Incidentally, the same holds true for using raw eggs. The USDA warns that we might expect one case of salmonella per 238,500 eggs. If you were lucky enough to have eighty lifetimes, you could get sick from eating an infected egg just once! You don't need even one case. Use fresh eggs. Keep them cold. But there's no way to make your own mayonnaise or aïoli without raw eggs. And millions of people have been eating those good things for thousands of years all over the world.

It's true that the way we cook has changed. We needn't squat in front of an open fire unless we choose to, and it may be difficult to track down a clay oven. But all that having been said, we can still abide by the Biblical injunction to share our food —it tastes better in company as we remember:

When thou cuttest down thine harvest in thine field, and has forgot a sheaf in the field, thou shalt not go again to fetch it; it shall be for the stranger, for the fatherless, and for the widow: that the Lord thy God may bless thee in all the work of thine hands. When thou beatest thine olive tree, thou shalt not go over the boughs again: it shall be for the stranger, for the fatherless, and for the widow. When thou gatherest the grapes at thy vineyard, thou shalt not glean it afterward: it shall be for the stranger, for the fatherless, and for the widow. And thou shalt re-member that thou wast a bondman in the land of Egypt: therefore I command thee to do this thing.

(Deuteronomy 24:19-22)

A variety of traditional food, well prepared, eaten in pleasant circum-stances, seasoned with generosity:

For as the rain cometh down, and the snow from heaven, and returneth not thither, but watereth the earth, and maketh it bring forth and bud, that it may give seed to the sower, and bread to the eater: So shall my word be that goeth forth out of my mouth: it shall not return unto me void, but it shall accomplish that which I please, and it shall prosper in the thing whereto I sent it. For ye shall go out with joy, and be led forth with peace: the moun-tains and the hills shall break forth before you into singing, and all the trees of the field shall clap their hands. Instead of the thorn shall come up the fir tree, and instead of the brier shall come up the myrtle tree: and it shall be to the Lord for a name, for an everlasting sign that shall not be cut off.

(Isaiah 56:10-13)

And we remember the advice given by the Chinese who, while not geo-graphically Biblical, existed at the same time and are respected for having their fair share of wisdom: "If you would be happy for a week take a wife; if you would be happy for a month kill a pig; but if you would be happy all your life, plant a garden."

These recipes, unless otherwise noted, serve six. Individual taste dic-tates how much salt and/or pepper to add to a dish. Because we would rather err on the side of too little rather than too much, we leave the exact amount to you. Salt and pepper can always be added by the judicious cook or at the table.

And finally, may none of your offerings be burnt. And may they bring you naught but joy.

> *Abide in me, and I in you. As the branch cannot bear fruit of itself, except it abide in the vine, no more can ye, except ye abide in me.*

(John 15:4)

Chapter One

HERBS and SPICES

 *And she came to Jerusalem with a very great train, with camels that bare spices, and very much gold, and precious stones: and when she was come to Solomon, she communed with him of all that was in her heart. And she gave the king an hundred and twenty talents of gold, and of spices very great store, and precious stones: there came no more such abundance of spices as these which the queen of Sheba gave to King Solomon.*

(I Kings 10:2,10)

Herbs and spices, the gemstones of the culinary world!

What's the difference between them? Herbs are plants with distinctly flavored leaves, which can be used fresh or dried in small amounts. (In recipes calling for herbs, a general rule is: 1 tbsp. fresh = 1 tsp. dried.)

In the earliest Assyrian and Babylonian gardens various herbs were grown including sesame, basil, coriander, dill, mint, thyme, bay, fennel, and sage.

Spices are aromatic parts of plants, which are dried, generally pulverized, and used in food preparation. A spice may be from the root, bark, fruit, flower, bud, or seed of the plant.

His cheeks are as a bed of spices, as sweet flowers: his lips like lilies, dropping sweet smelling myrrh.

(Song of Solomon 5:13)

Around 2600 B.C. Egyptian records describe spices used for cooking and perfumery as well as those useful in the concoction of medicines. When the treatment didn't work, spices were then incorporated as embalming ingredients to clean and rinse the abdominal cavity before mummification.

The ancients also used spices and aromatic gums as anointing oils and incense to banish evil spirits and to get rid of unpleasant odors, insects, pests, and serpents.

> *Awake, O north wind; and come, thou south; blow upon my garden, that the spices thereof may flow out. Let my beloved come into his garden, and eat his pleasant fruits.*
> (Song of Solomon 4:16)

Large quantities of spices blew into Egypt's gardens from Arabia and Palestine, and by the time the trade routes extended to Rome, the list of herbs and spices used to cook dishes for upper-class tables had grown enormously. Apparently, the aristocracy ate nothing without a covering sauce or dressing. In addition to the imported spices, their gardeners grew many herbs and spices locally. These included anise, cinnamon, coriander, cumin, mustard, saffron, savory, lovage, sesame seed and rue, poppy seeds, and parsley.

> *But woe unto you, Pharisees! for ye tithe mint and rue and all manner of herbs, and pass over judgment and the love of God: these ought ye to have done, and not to leave the other undone.*
> (Luke 11:42)

But long before the Romans:

> *All the heave offerings of the holy things, which the children of Israel offer unto the Lord, have I given thee, and thy sons and thy daughters with thee, by a statute for ever: it is a covenant of salt for ever before the Lord unto thee and to thy seed with thee.*
> (Numbers 18:19)

What is that covenant of salt? Is it the belief that when one person ate another person's food, he came under the man's protection? The symbol of hospitality, friendship, honesty? Or is it something more?

Let your speech be alway with grace, seasoned with salt, that ye may know how ye ought to answer every man.

(Colossians 4:6)

Salt, the most widespread condiment of all times, is intimately connected with the most important step in mankind's progress — going from nomadic wandering, dependent on an almost exclusive animal food diet to living in agricultural stability, harvesting vegetables and cereals for sustenance.

Agrarian societies needed the salt more than their hunting forefathers. Meat (blood) contains salt; cereals are unpalatable without it. The gods were worshipped for lavishing the fruits of the earth on humans, early man made offerings of valued foodstuffs to keep those good things coming, and it was over these sacrifices that covenants were sealed.

And every oblation of thy meat offering shalt thou season with salt; neither shalt thou suffer the salt of the covenant of thy God to be lacking from thy meat offering: with all thine offerings thou shalt offer salt.

(Leviticus 2:13)

Again and again they tell us — nothing was valued more highly than salt. Even though it was plentiful in Bible lands, it was still a precious commodity as a seasoning and method to preserve meat and fish, essential to the health of man and livestock. The Dead Sea was called the Salt Sea for good reason. It is the saltiest body of water in the world, and salt mining has been going on in that region for at least five thousand years.

Can the fig tree, my brethren, bear olive berries? either a vine, figs? so can no fountain both yield salt water and fresh.

(James 3:12)

Ancient highways of commerce were built on salt. One of the oldest roads in Italy is the Via Salaria, used to transport salt from the salt pans of Ostia, the ancient port of Rome. Cakes of salt have been used as currency. In the Roman army, an allowance of salt was made, called a *salarium*, which later was converted to somebody's paycheck.

Herodotus described the caravan route uniting Libyan salt oases. The salt of Palmyra was an important element in the trade between the Syrian ports and the Persian Gulf.

Salt lasts. When people share a meal, breaking bread and salting food together, they create a vow of enduring camaraderie. To eat the king's salt meant to owe him undying loyalty.

> *Ye are the salt of the earth: but if the salt have lost his savour, wherewith shall it be salted? it is thenceforth good for nothing, but to be cast out, and to be trodden under foot of men.*
>
> (Matthew 5:13)

About seventy-five percent of salt is sodium chloride. The rest consists of calcium, magnesium, carbon, sulfur, potassium, and trace elements.

Although salt is used primarily to enhance the flavor of foods, today there is some concern about its overuse. Too much constricts blood vessels, making the heart work harder. Salt dehydrates blood cells and vessels, causing shrinkage of the tissues, and an excess can clog the kidneys. However, salt in moderate amounts allows the blood vessels to contract enough to maintain body warmth and good intestinal muscle tone. Besides:

> *Can that which is unsavoury be eaten without salt? or is there any taste in the white of an egg?*
>
> (Job 6:6)

For those who must limit their salt intake, various substitutions have been proposed, including the use of palatable herbs. The ancients were way ahead of us there, too.

The mint family includes more than 3,000 species. It grows wild in the Holy Land along ditches and stream banks and in swamps.

The Greeks called it *mintha*, which was later latinized to *mentha*. The Romans rubbed it into their tables before they sat down (or reclined) at a banquet.

A perennial herb grown for its aromatic leaves, three varieties were known to Bible people: peppermint, with bright green leaves and purplish stems; spearmint, with a more delicate flavor, light gray-green leaves; and pennyroyal, with stems lying on the ground and small bluish-lavender flowers.

Mint was commonly used as a condiment because of its aromatic oil.

Pennyroyal, grown in the herb garden, is said to keep mosquitoes away. Any mint repels field mice. Medicinally, mint leaves were crushed and steeped in infusions for headaches, general pain, and especially for their soothing effect on the stomach.

The essential oils are strongest when mint is flowering. This is the time to gather the leaves and dry them for later use. Mint is a natural with lamb either as a sauce or in mint jelly. It makes a pleasant tea or it can be crushed over fruit salads, cooked with vegetables, or used as a flavoring in sherbets, cake frostings, and chocolate desserts.

> *Woe unto you, scribes and Pharisees, hypocrites! for ye pay tithe of mint and anise . . . and have omitted the weightier matters of the law, judgment, mercy, and faith: these ought ye to have done, and not to leave the other undone.*
>
> (Matthew 23:23)

Matthew underscores Luke's warning in almost the same words. Later translators substituted dill for anise. According to the scholars, the anise mentioned in the Bible is really dill.

Dill then (Anethum graveolens) has been grown in Bible countries since ancient times. It's a hardy annual of the carrot family, which escapes to the wild every chance it gets. Maybe because it hates being called anise! Dill is used to flavor soups, salads, and sauces, and its leaves and seeds (actually the dried fruit) have seasoned many a crock of pickles.

Its Anglo-Saxon word comes from "*dili*," which means to lull to sleep. Dill water was used to send our ancestors' babies to rock-a-bye land. The dill water was a good idea. It's been known through the ages for its ability to soothe and benefit digestion in older children as well as adults.

But despite what scholars said about anise being dill (and vice versa), there are references to anise being indigenous to Asia Minor, Egypt, and the Greek Islands. It was mentioned in early Egyptian writings, and anise seeds have been found in Greek ruins dating back to 1500 B.C.

The Sumerians, even earlier, left records of both anise (Pimpinella anisum) and its close relative, fennel (Foeniculum vulgare). In the First Century A.D., the Roman writer, Pliny, remarked: "Anise serves well for seasoning all meats; and the kitchen cannot get along without it."

Apparently, they couldn't do without fennel, either. Not only was it thrown into the cooking pot, fennel, a sacred herb, was one of the leaves used to crown victorious Roman heroes.

Members of the same botanical family, umbelliferae (carrot and parsley), aromatic anise, and fennel seed emit the familiar licorice-like flavor. The ground powder or tiny, whole seeds were used to flavor bread and rolls, cookies, sauces, sweet puddings, creams, cakes, and candies. They still are. Chewed after a meal, the seeds freshen the breath and aid the digestion.

If a meal today includes a chicken or meat stew, chances are it will be flavored with a bay leaf — and if it's grown in California, use sparingly, no more than a sixth of a dried leaf — it's a very potent herb.

> *I have seen the wicked in great power, and spreading himself like a green bay tree.*
>
> (Psalms 37:35)

In the above selection the Hebrew word is "*Ezrah*," the only time this word is translated "bay tree." Everywhere else in the Bible, the word is rendered "native." Therefore, it might be reasonable to assume that the bay tree (Laurus nobilis) is indigenous to and grew strongly in the Holy Land.

The tree reaches fifty feet or more and has large, dark green, aromatic leaves, greenish-yellow flowers, and shiny black berries that were (and are) used in soups, meats, and fish and always in a *bouquet garni*.

One of the oldest spices known and one of the most familiar to us is cinnamon, used in ancient temples and as an ingredient in holy anointing oils.

> *And when the sabbath was past, Mary Magdalene, and Mary the mother of James, and Salome, had bought sweet spices, that they might come and anoint him.*
>
> (Mark 16:1)

The cinnamon tree (Cinnamomum zeyllanicum), another member of the laurel family, is evergreen and small, with long, stiff leaves. The pale yellow flowers are grouped in silky clusters. The versatile bark, sold in sticks or ground to powder, provides the familiar heavenly scent. It is sweet, mildly pungent and aromatic.

Today, most of what we call cinnamon is actually cassia (Cinnamomum cassia), which was a spice of the Scriptures, a precious perfume and one of the ingredients of the holy oils. The oil is obtained by steam distillation of the plants, leaves, twigs, and immature fruits called cassia buds. Cassia powder is stronger than cinnamon and darker in color.

Either cinnamon or cassia is used in beverages, fruits, pastries, cakes, cookies, and rainy day cinnamon toast we remember from when we were children.

Another familiar flavor from childhood gingerbread men (or women) is coriander.

 *And the house of Israel called the name thereof Manna: and it was like coriander seed, white; and the taste of it was like wafers made with honey.*

(Exodus 16:31)

An annual herb of the carrot family native to the Holy Land, the coriander's (Coriandrum sativum) fruits are globular and brown to yellowish-red. All parts of the plant have a strong odor. The whole seed is used in pickling. In its ground form, it is used to flavor bread, pastries, and candy. The leaves are useful in soups, puddings, curries, and wines, while the oil is added to perfume, chocolate, and liqueurs.

Another herb is obliquely described in the Bible:

Also when they shall be afraid of that which is high, and fears shall be in the way, and the almond tree shall flourish, and the grasshopper shall be a burden, and desire shall fail: because man goeth to his long home, and the mourners go about the streets: . . . Then shall the dust return to the earth as it was: and the spirit shall return unto God who gave it.

(Ecclesiastes 12:5,7)

Oblique? That seems to be a rather straightforward account of advancing age, especially the part about dwindling desire. But before we jump to the obvious conclusion, in Bible times the pickled buds of capers (Capparis spinosa) were thought to stimulate taste and appetite, adding *desire* to food. In the above quotation taken from the King James version of Ecclesiastes, the translation is "desire shall fail," but the original Hebrew says that the *caper berry* shall fail.

The caper bush is a deciduous, spiny shrub of straggling habit about three feet high, valued for its flower buds, which are pickled and sold as capers. If allowed to flower, the buds open to white blossoms with magenta-purple stamens, yellow-tipped, in the center of wide-open petals.

The Romans were such epicures, they hardly let the caper buds open, but the herb they doted on more than any other was cumin.

> *For the fitches are not threshed with a threshing instru-*
> *ment, neither is a cart wheel turned about upon the cum-*
> *min; but the fitches are beaten out with a staff, and the*
> *cummin with a rod.*
>
> (Isaiah 28:27)

The Romans used cumin (Cuminum cyminum) in so many foods, it was practically their universal herb. They sprinkled it on oysters and shell-fish, in sausage, in the cooking water for beets and cabbages, in barley soup, roasts, and in stews of lentils, peas, and beans. In case such a long list brings on a condition of fits, cumin was also used as an antispasmodic. Its oil is an ingredient of perfume.

Native to the Middle East, cumin is an annual herb with an erect stem and tiny white or rose flowers. The small elliptical, hairy fruits contain grains — aromatic seeds very similar in taste to caraway seeds — that are ground and used to flavor bread, soups, chutney, and curry as well as other dishes like stewed meats, sauerkraut, and sausage, all of which would hardly be palatable without mustard.

> *It is like a grain of mustard seed, which a man took, and*
> *cast into his garden; and it grew, and waxed a great tree;*
> *and the fowls of the air lodged in the branches of it.*
>
> (Luke 13:19)

The Sumerians raised mustard (Brassica nigra) that even now grows wild in the Holy Land. During spring, whole meadows are yellow with the lemon-colored blooms. The leaves, a rich, dark green with a downy sur-face, are prepared as a vegetable and are thought to be very healthful. The seeds, of course, are tiny.

> *And Jesus said unto them, Because of your unbelief: for*
> *verily I say unto you, If ye have faith as a grain of mus-*
> *tard seed, ye shall say unto this mountain, Remove hence*
> *to yonder place; and it shall remove; and nothing shall*
> *be impossible unto you.*
>
> (Matthew 17:20)

Mustard is used to flavor meat and cheese dishes and to make poultices for chest colds. The whole seeds have practically no odor until they are crushed and a little water is added. Then they give off a sharp, piercing scent.

Apicius has handed down a recipe in which crushed mustard seeds are prepared with vinegar, then mixed with ground pine kernels and almonds.

The annual herb Brassica nigra is the black mustard, the tallest member of its family, whose ground-up seeds produce commercial mustard. The Brassica family includes cabbage, kale, broccoli, cauliflower, brussels sprouts, and collards.

> *Another parable put he forth unto them, saying, The kingdom of heaven is like to a grain of mustard seed, which a man took, and sowed in his field: which indeed is the least of all seeds: but when it is grown, it is the greatest among herbs, and becometh a tree, so that the birds of the air come and lodge in the branches thereof.*
>
> (Matthew 13:31-32)

In Bible lands saffron (Crocus sativus) was used as an ingredient in many of the complicated medicines, in coloring foods, and as a fabric dye.

Valued ever since, saffron is a corm of the Iris family, a bulbous herb that blooms in autumn before its leaves appear. The delicately scented flowers are a rosy lavender with vivid orange stigmas. It is the dried stigmas that produce the costly orange powder. In cooking, it should be used in very small quantities to impart its subtle but characteristic flavor.

> *Spikenard and saffron; calamus and cinnamon, with all trees of frankincense; myrrh and aloes, with all the chief spices:*
>
> (Song of Solomon 4:14)

Saffron was strewn in Greek halls, courts, theatres, and in the Roman baths. When Nero made his entry into Rome, the streets were sprinkled with saffron, long considered a royal color.

Since it takes four thousand blossoms to make an ounce, that must have been some parade!

Recipes using salt, herbs and spices are not given in this space since they are used throughout in recipes that follow in every chapter.

Chapter Two

SOUP

Although the Bible does not mention soup specifically, it is inconceivable that the earliest cooks didn't throw together ingredients they had on hand and heat them with water in whatever they could devise as a soup pot. Refinements continued, probably daily.

Pottage (also spelled potage) is defined as a stew or thick soup of meat and/or vegetables.

> *And Esau said to Jacob, Feed me, I pray thee, with that same red pottage; for I am faint . . .*
>
> (Genesis 25:30)

And we all know he sold his birthright for a mess of it. (Incidentally, the ancients called many things red that were any shade of brown.)

Soups ranged from plain cut-up vegetables simmered in water to some version of cream soups. Barley and lentils thickened soups. So did every kind of wheat. Meat soups included organs and, not to put it too delicately, offal. Cream soups not only had milk or cream added, but egg yolk as well. Somewhere along the way ancient cooks undoubtedly made soup stock from leftover meat or fish, bones, vegetables, herbs, and water. Most cooks have their favorite stock recipes. In case you don't, we include some basic ones along with the warning that they are not to be taken too seriously in terms of amounts or ingredients. Use what you have; that's the whole idea.

It is just as important today, as it was then, to taste the soup. Adjust the seasonings. Consider adding sautéed onions and/or garlic, possibly lemon juice. To thicken the soup, a bit of flour mixed with cold water, then added to the soup will help. So will a roux of butter cooked with a little flour for five minutes, then whisked into the soup; or a portion of the vegetables taken out and blended in the blender.

You can make the soup look attractive by adding a topping of grated cheese, minced spring onions, or chives, any colorful slivered vegetable, roasted nuts, seeds, or croutons.

BASIC VEGETABLE STOCK

2 tbsp. olive oil
½ cup chopped onion
2 cloves garlic
½ tsp. salt
   bouquet garni*
¼ cup each carrots, turnips, parsnips
2 cups diced celery, including leaves
1 cup shredded romaine or other dark green lettuce

*Bouquet garni: Tie in a square of cheesecloth: 3 or 4 sprigs parsley, 1 tbsp. each thyme, dill, anise, and fennel, ½ bay leaf.

In large soup pot, sauté onion and garlic in olive oil. Add the rest of the ingredients and enough cold water to cover. Bring to a boil. Partly cover and simmer about 1½ hours until the vegetables are very tender. Strain.

Use right away as a soup base or chill (even freeze) for future use.

BEEF STOCK

6 lbs. small to medium shin and marrow bones
4 quarts water
½ bay leaf
1 tsp. thyme
3 sprigs parsley
1 large diced carrot
3 stalks of celery, diced
1 medium diced onion

Preheat oven to 350°.
Brown bones in the oven.
When browned, place them in a large stockpot with the remaining ingredients. Bring to a boil. Reduce heat and simmer, uncovered, for 3 hours or until the liquid is reduced by half. Strain stock. Cool and refrigerate or freeze whatever portion is not used right away for soup.

CHICKEN STOCK

4   lbs. chicken backs, necks, and wings
     boiling water to cover
4   quarts cold water
½   bay leaf
1   tsp. each of thyme, cinnamon, dill, anise, and fennel
6   stems of parsley
1   medium onion, diced
3   stalks of celery, diced
1   medium diced carrot

Pour the boiling water (not the 4 quarts) over the chicken parts. Drain and discard water.

Bring the chicken parts slowly to a boil in the 4 quarts of water with the rest of the ingredients. Reduce the heat and simmer 2½ to 3 hours or until reduced by half. Strain stock and cool.

ESAU'S RED LENTIL SOUP

4 cups water
4 cups vegetable or meat stock
2 cups red lentils
1 onion
2 stalks of celery
2 cloves of garlic
2 tbsp. olive oil
3 tsp. salt

Bring water to boil. Add lentils and simmer until soft (about 30 minutes). Meanwhile, halve, then slice the onion into crescents and slice the garlic and celery. Quickly sauté in oil until brown. Add salt to soup. Stir in sautéed onions and garlic and taste again, adjusting seasoning. Simmer all together for 15 minutes.

. . . the Lord said unto Gideon, Every one that lappeth of the water with his tongue, as a dog lappeth, him shalt thou set by himself; likewise every one that boweth down upon his knees to drink. And the number of them that lapped, putting their hand to their mouth, were three hundred men: but all the rest of the people bowed down upon their knees to drink water. And the Lord said unto Gideon, By the three hundred men that lapped will I save you, and deliver the Midianites into thine hand: and let all the other people go every man unto his place.

(Judges 7:5-7)

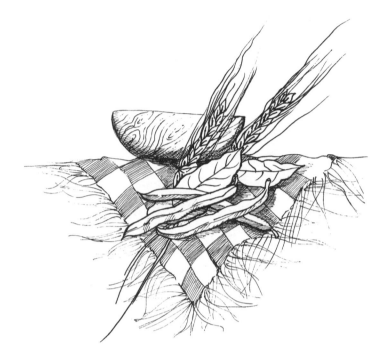

GIDEON'S BARLEY SOUP

    1   chopped onion
    3   cloves garlic
    2   tbsp. olive oil
1½ quarts water
    1   quart vegetable stock
    1   cup barley
    ½   bay leaf
    2   carrots
    2   stalks celery
1½ cups chopped green beans
    1   tsp. basil
    1   tbsp. salt
        salt and pepper to taste

In a large soup pot, sauté onions, celery and garlic in olive oil. When they are tender and beginning to brown, add the water and stock and bring to a boil.

Rinse barley under running water. Add to boiling soup. Add bay leaf and simmer until barley is tender, about one hour. Add carrots and green beans, basil, and salt. Cook until vegetables are just tender. Taste and add more salt and pepper if desired.

AROMATIC FENNEL SOUP

1   medium fennel bulb
¼   cup olive oil
2   large onions, chopped
4   cloves of garlic, minced
1   tsp. orange zest*
1   cup chopped orange
    salt and ground pepper to taste
6   cups water
1½ cups cooked chickpeas

*We use the term "zest" throughout these recipes to mean the scraped citrus peel obtained with the use of a special zesting tool, finer than chopped or minced.

This soup may be made a day ahead and reheated at the last minute.

Remove fennel fronds, mince, and put aside. Cut off and discard the stems and trim the root end. Cut the bulb in half lengthwise. Place it cut side down on a cutting board and slice into thin, long strips. Set this aside separately from the fronds.

Heat the olive oil in a large soup kettle. Add onions and garlic and sauté until translucent. Add the orange zest and cook another two minutes. Stir in the chopped orange, cook an additional two or three minutes.

Add the fennel slices and cook, stirring occasionally until they soften. Season with salt and pepper to taste.

Add the water and bring to a boil. Simmer, stirring from time to time, until the fennel is tender, approximately fifteen minutes.

Add the chickpeas. Simmer another five minutes and adjust the seasonings. Garnish individual soup bowls with fennel fronds. Serve hot.

And it came to pass, when David was come to Mahanaim, that Shobi the son of Nahash of Rabbah of the children of Ammon, and Machir the son of Ammiel of Lodebar, and Barzillai the Gileadite of Rogelim, Brought beds, and basons, and earthen vessels, and wheat, and barley, and flour, and parched corn, and beans, and lentiles, and parched pulse . . .

(II Samuel 17:27-28)

BARZILLAI, THE GILEADITE'S ONION SOUP

2   large onions, sliced
2   tbsp. butter
1   tbsp. flour
1   cup dry white wine
5   pints chicken (or vegetable) stock
    salt and pepper to taste
    toasted slices of sourdough or French bread,
        about ½" thick, cut into croutons
2   oz. grated Swiss cheese

Cook onions slowly in a large saucepan with the butter until golden. Add flour, stir and cook a few minutes. Add wine, stock, salt, and pepper. Bring to a boil, then reduce heat and simmer gently forty-five minutes.

When ready to serve, turn into an ovenproof casserole, float toasted croutons on top that were sautéed in extra butter. Sprinkle with grated cheese. Place under broiler until the cheese melts and browns.

Thus Melzar took away the portion of their meat, and the wine that they should drink; and gave them pulse. As for these four children, God gave them knowledge and skill in all learning and wisdom: and Daniel had understanding in all visions and dreams.

(Daniel 1:16-17)

VEGETABLE BARLEY SOUP MELZAR

½ cup barley, soaked overnight in water
1 cup each chickpeas, lentils, and dried green split peas
10 cups water
2 tbsp. olive oil
2 heads of leeks, chopped
2 celery stalks, chopped
½ tsp. each coriander and oregano
  pinch each of anise and fennel
4 grape leaves chopped (optional)
½ tsp. honey

Discard barley water and rinse. Into a large soup pot, put first six ingredients. Cook gently over low heat at least 3 hours. During the last half hour, add the seasonings. Stir. Simmer ½ hour.

And Elisha came again to Gilgal: and there was a dearth in the land; and the sons of the prophets were sitting before him: and he said unto his servant, Set on the great pot and seethe pottage for the sons of the prophets. And one went out into the field to gather herbs, and found a wild vine, and gathered thereof wild gourds his lap full, and came and shred them into the pot of pottage: for they knew them not.

(II Kings 4:38-39)

CHICKPEA SOUP DAVID

1   cup chickpeas (garbanzo beans), soaked overnight
     juice of 2 lemons
2   cloves crushed garlic
1   large sliced carrot
2   pints stock or water
1   tbsp. chopped parsley
     salt and freshly ground black pepper

Drain the water the chickpeas soaked in and discard. Use fresh water to cover. Bring to a boil. Change again to fresh water or stock. Add the sliced carrot. Simmer until tender. Purée with lemon juice and garlic in food processor or blender. Blend in a ladleful of stock. Heat gently, adjust seasoning and serve garnished with parsley. A trickle of olive oil may be added at the table. It's optional.

BEAN SOUP ELISHA

This is a basic recipe for lentils, dried beans, or split peas. It can be used as a base for other soups. Note that the beans must be soaked overnight.

    1   chopped onion
    1   chopped celery stalk
    4   cloves of garlic, minced
    2   tbsp. olive oil
 1½   quarts water
    1   quart vegetable stock
    1   tsp. sage
    ½   bay leaf
 2½   cups dried beans, soaked overnight
        salt and pepper to taste

Thickener

    4   tbsp. oil
    ¼   cup flour
    2   cups water

Heat olive oil in a large soup pot, then sauté onions, celery and garlic until golden. Add stock and water, bay leaf, and sage. Bring to a boil. Wash and sort beans, add to water, and bring to a boil again. Simmer gently until tender, which could be anywhere from 2 to 4 hours, depending on the kind of bean. The longer this soup cooks, the better it tastes and the less it needs a thickener.

To thicken soup, heat oil in a small saucepan, add flour and cook slowly for 5 minutes, stirring occasionally. Add water and salt and bring to a boil, stirring constantly. Pour into soup.

Or bind the soup by spooning about a quarter of the beans into a blender along with some broth. Purée, then return to the soup.

It should be thick, but not stiff. Add more water or stock as needed. Taste, adding salt and pepper.

EGG LEMON SOUP ATHENAEUS

2 quarts chicken stock
1 cup cooked barley
2 shallots, minced
4 eggs, room temperature
   juice of 2 lemons
1 tbsp. fennel leaves, minced
   strips of thin lemon peel
   salt to taste

Bring stock to boil in a large saucepan. Add barley and shallots, cover, reduce heat and let simmer for 20 minutes.

In the meantime, have 2 bowls ready — a medium size and a small one. Separate the eggs, putting the whites into the larger bowl and the yolks into the smaller. Beat whites until soft peaks form. Whisk the yolks until blended, then slowly fold them into the whites. Gradually add the lemon juice, beating constantly.

Remove the stock from the heat. Slowly ladle 2 cups of stock into the beaten eggs, whisking continuously. Pour egg mixture into the stock saucepan, place over low heat, stirring. Do not boil. Add fennel leaves and salt to taste. Garnish with lemon strips twisted into curls. Serve.

EGG LEMON SOUP DAPHNI

7   cups chicken or vegetable stock
3   cloves roasted garlic (see Chapter 3 for recipe)
1   cup barley
5   eggs
    juice of 3 large lemons
    salt to taste
    thin lemon slices
½   cup chopped fresh parsley

Bring the stock to a boil and add the garlic and barley. Simmer until the barley is just tender, about 20 minutes. Remove and discard the garlic. Lower the heat.

Just before serving, beat the eggs lightly, then beat in some of the lemon juice. Stir a ladleful of the hot stock into the egg mixture, beating constantly. Return the mixture to the remaining stock, stirring. Turn off the heat. The soup must not boil or the eggs will curdle. Season to taste. Add rest of lemon juice. Serve garnished with lemon slices and chopped parsley.

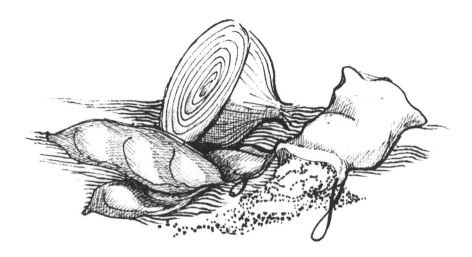

BENJAMIN'S BARLEY SOUP

1¼ cups barley, unpearled
10 cups vegetable stock
 1 onion, chopped
10 oz. canned fava beans
 1 cup parsley, chopped
 1 bay leaf
 ¼ cup mint, chopped
1½ tsp. marjoram
    salt and pepper to taste

Cook barley, bay leaf, and marjoram in vegetable stock in a large covered pot over medium heat for 45 minutes. Add beans and parsley and simmer another 15 minutes. Add mint, salt and pepper to taste, and leave on stove with heat turned off another five minutes.

LENTIL SOUP AMALIA

1 lb. lentils
   olive oil
2 medium onions, chopped
3 stalks celery, chopped
2 small carrots, chopped
2 cloves garlic, minced
½ bay leaf
1 tsp. dried oregano
   salt to taste
½ cup red wine

    Rinse and pick over lentils. Warm some olive oil in a large soup pot over medium heat. Sauté until onions are limp (5 minutes), then add lentils and water to cover by about 3 inches. Add everything but salt and wine. Bring to a boil. Cover, reduce heat and simmer until the lentils are tender (about 30 minutes). Check now and then to be sure they are covered with water. Add more water if needed.

    Remove from stove and discard the bay leaf. Season with salt and wine. Cover and let stand a few minutes, then serve.

Chapter Three

VEGETABLES

 And God said, Behold, I have given you every herb bearing seed, which is upon the face of all the earth, and every tree, in the which is the fruit of a tree yielding seed; to you it shall be for meat.

(Genesis 1:29)

Globe artichokes (Cynara scolymus), herbaceous perennials of the thistle family were prized several centuries before Christ.

Thorns also and thistles shall it bring forth to thee; and thou shalt eat the herb of the field.

(Genesis 3:18)

The edible parts, of course, are the fleshy bases of the immature flower heads and the tender ends of the bracts. In ancient times the young, blanched leaves rather than the flower heads were eaten.

Ye shall know them by their fruits. Do men gather grapes of thorns, or figs of thistles?

(Matthew 7:16)

Like asparagus and broccoli, artichokes are edible only when they are immature (otherwise, you might just as well be nibbling on thorns). That's when the bracts are unblemished, closed tightly toward the top, and closely overlaid one upon another; with bright, vibrant color. At the market, pass up the larger artichokes with loose, open bracts in favor of those about the size of a large lemon.

They may be steamed whole and served with garlic aïoli. (In our opinion, almost anything can.) How in the world did the first gourmet know what to eat? We're luckier — experienced artichoke lovers have left detailed instructions, weird as they sound to the novice. Start with the outer leaves and work toward the center, tearing off each leaf, dipping the wider fleshy part in sauce, then scraping it off against your teeth. In the center of the artichoke is a lighter green cone of tender leaves that can be removed in one piece with a curved grapefruit knife. Beneath this is the prickly "choke," which is inedible. The part known as the "heart" is just below. It is the center of the artichoke and contains the most intense flavor.

Carrots (Daucus carota sativa) are classified as biennial herbs whose cultivated forms developed from the wild carrot which was thin and wiry and appeared unpromising as a source of food. But it was one of the herbs that responded quickly, improving with cultivation and has, therefore, been grown in the Mediterranean area ever since several centuries before the Christian Era.

It does not, strictly speaking, appear in the Bible as carrot. The Bible isn't specific about individual vegetables, referring to most of them as herbs. We learn from Greek and Roman (and earlier Mesopotamian and Egyptian) records that these included celery, asparagus, and beets although they were most likely primitive varieties of the versions we know.

If you grow carrots in your garden, an old tip for the slow-sprouting seeds is to mix them with radish seeds, which pop up quickly, marking the row. By the time the carrot seedlings appear, the radishes are ready to be pulled, leaving plenty of room for the carrots to mature.

Seed catalogs advise that flavor varies considerably depending on the variety and also from soil to soil. As to the first, experiment with different types until you find one to your liking; enrich the soil with lots of compost. That will also help to keep the soil friable — carrots do best in pulverized situations where they won't encounter any stones.

Celery (Apium graveolens) is native to the near east and eastern Mediterranean area and was known to the Greeks and Romans, but perhaps not much earlier since we don't find mention of it in very ancient languages. It was used mainly as a flavoring and for quite a long time as a medicinal herb. Closer to modern times celery stalks were blanched, but recently growers are cultivating the natural green and more stringless bunches.

We remember the fish, which we did eat in Egypt freely; and the cucumbers . . .

(Numbers 11:5)

Cucumbers (Cucumis sativus) grew around the shores of Lake Karun when the pyramids were being built and in the garden of Ur-Nammu at Ur around 2100 B.C.

Beaumont and Fletcher, who came along quite a bit later, referred to certain women as cold as cucumbers in their play *Cupid's Revenge* in 1610 and that may be where "cool as a cucumber" entered the language.

In 1970 scientists with thermometers proved once and for all what ordinary folks knew for centuries — that cucumbers are really cool. The inside of a cucumber on a warm day registers about 20° cooler than the air.

The ancients, as usual, knew all about it. Throughout their hot climates, they planted cucumbers to cool off generations of royalty as well as commoners.

Cucumis are classified as trailing or tendril-climbing annual herbs grown for their immature, green fruits. They belong to the same extended family as gourds, squashes, pumpkins, and melons, all of which have separate male and female flowers. They are nearly all vines that climb by means of sensitive tendrils that twist tightly around anything in their path. We usually think of gourds as inedible, melons as sweet, and the others as edible but not sweet. The ancients were familiar with various types, but it is impossible to say which of their varieties correspond with ours. We will, therefore, in a move towards accuracy, confine our recipes to cucumbers (in the chapter on salads) and melons (under desserts) and omit both summer and winter squash.

The juice of cucumbers has been used for centuries to keep the skin soft and as a soothing lotion for burned or irritated skin. Withered or shriveled cucumbers are tough and bitter. Avoid them.

The traditional method of making pickles was to cook together cucumbers, apple cider or white wine vinegar, dill, water, garlic, and kosher salt in an earthenware crock, weight down the lid, and wait for weeks while the area close to the operation took on the aroma of an open jar of pickles. When the pickles were inspected, they were either great or spoiled — another culinary risk.

If you really want to get into this method, the U.S. Government Printing Office, Washington, D.C. has a free booklet on the subject, which improves the odds.

It's hard to believe, but some folks still avoid garlic (Allium sativum) and to a lesser extent, onions — whether for olfactory reasons or because garlic has a working class reputation. Now why doesn't that apply to leeks?

Garlic is a hardy perennial bulb, a member of the same Allium family as onions and leeks — the ancients knew all three. Garlic alone separates beneath a papery skin into cloves, which are used to flavor meats, dressings, and sauces.

Garlic was mentioned in Sanskrit over five thousand years ago and was a staple in the ancient Sumerian diet. They raised it in the Tigris-Euphrates valley before 2000 B.C. Slaves in Egypt ate it as a cooked vegetable. Indeed, it has been said that the laborers who built the pyramids subsisted largely on garlic, leeks, and onions along with sour wine.

Homer praised garlic for its health-giving properties. Greek physicians Hippocrates and Dioscorides used alliums to treat insect bites, worms, coughs, menstrual disorders, skin diseases, and epilepsy. Both Greek and Roman soldiers relied on garlic for strength and courage before going into battle as well as an aphrodisiac (presumably if they were victorious). Our old friend, Pliny, came up with sixty-one garlic cures for everything from coughs to wild animal bites, madness to diminished libido. According to this ancient Roman, the garlic remedy can be administered in honey, wine, or flavored with coriander, but he also warns that the treatment may result in flatulence and/or thirst. Nevertheless, the great Roman physician, Galen, lauded garlic as the "medicine of the poor" presumably because they couldn't afford health insurance.

In antiquity, garlic was commonly referred to as a "cure-all" and it was prescribed for hundreds of specific ailments including infections, high blood pressure, tuberculosis, influenza, toothache, and the common cold. Its reputation has persisted ever since. It has been praised as a preventative against the plague and to cure cases of nervous illness. In Balkan countries garlic was rubbed on doorknobs and window frames to keep out vampires.

Bolivian Indians swear that a bull will not charge anyone who carries garlic. Then there's the old belief that a magnet rubbed with garlic loses its power.

Today, there is more scientific evidence that garlic has remarkable properties. It is classified as a digestive, stimulant, diuretic, and antispasmodic agent. It contains a natural antibiotic, and modern researchers have learned that an extract of garlic in a test tube does indeed kill tuberculosis bacteria; and in as low a concentration as ten parts per million, destroys 98 percent of mosquito larvae.

Planted near roses, garlic helps to ward off aphids and Japanese beetles. Companionate planting holds that the emanations, odors, and juices of certain plants act as repellents to various insects, just as mothballs ward off moths. In medieval castles, furs and woolen garments were hung in a place called the *garderobe* located next to the stone privy for similar reasons.

Eating garlic will lower cholesterol levels somewhat as will making lifestyle and dietary changes, and garlic has always been touted to repel vampires, which is more than you can say for exercise alone.

Buy garlic that feels firm and fresh, not dry and hollow. If you have a garden, plant some. It's the easiest thing in the world to grow. Separate the garlic cloves and plant in ordinary soil with the pointed tip facing up. Each single clove produces a head.

We offer the quote one more time because we have no other way to introduce leeks:

> *And the mixt multitude that was among them fell a lusting: and the children of Israel also wept again, and said, Who shall give us flesh to eat? We remember the fish, which we did eat in Egypt freely; the cucumbers, and the melons, and the leeks, and the onions, and the garlick:*
>
> (Numbers 11:4-5)

Leeks, for some reason, are considered the most valued of the triumvirate leek, garlic, and onion. Even in ancient times, the Egyptians esteemed it as a sacred plant. The leek (Allium porrum) has leaves that are more open than the other two and tends not to form a bulb at the base.

Although onions and, to a large extent, garlic were regarded as food for the poor, leeks were considered fit for an emperor. Nero, to be exact. In the first century A.D. he apparently consumed acres of them. According to Pliny, Nero ate leeks and oil to improve his voice. And we thought he was a fiddler.

A hearty biennial, leeks are even milder than green onions, grown for the lower part of its leaves which are white. The green part is eaten with salad, the bulb cooked as a vegetable and as seasoning.

Onions (Allium cepa) were grown in large quantities near the Nile. The Greek historian Herodotus says that when the Great Pyramid of Khufu was built, a huge sum was spent supplying the builders with onions, garlic, and radishes.

According to ancient authorities, Egyptians swore on the sacredness of garlic and onions. Indeed, the inhabitants of Pelusium, an old Egyptian city, worshipped the onion, but not garlic.

Today in the East people believe that eating onions keeps you from getting thirsty. Onion superstitions are persistent: hanging onions over doorways keeps out infections; placing a raw onion beneath the pillow on St. Thomas's Eve brings dreams of one's future spouse.

Onions, leeks, and garlic are members of the large lily family. They comprise approximately 600 species. Many were known in ancient Egypt as early as 3200 B.C., and even today we have a variety called "Egyptian onion" which is the Allium cepa of history. It produces bulbs at the top of the stem in contrast to other varieties which, of course, form bulbs under the soil and are harvested after the green tops die down.

Confused about scallions vs. green onions? They're the same — both are the green leaves of the immature plant, sometimes referred to as "bunch" onions. Scallion gets its name from Ascalon and means onion of Ascalon just as shallots (Allium ascalonicum) are named for the Biblical city of Ashkelon, referring to the same ancient city of Palestine twelve miles north of Gaza whose turbulent history reaches back to two thousand years before Christ.

Shallots have a very mild onion-garlic flavor. They are more like garlic than onions with a bulb made up of separate cloves.

> *Prove thy servants, I beseech thee, ten days: and let them give us pulse to eat, and water to drink.*
>
> (Daniel 1:12)

The common garden pea (Pisum sativum) has been found in the Near East dating back to 7000-6000 B.C., but amazingly, is nowhere mentioned in the Bible. Maybe they called it something else.

Pulses, often served with grains, are field peas, lentils, beans, and chickpeas. Peas and beans were grown by the Hittites, in Assyria, and in Babylon.

The Greeks even had a "god of Beans" and held a bean festival. Pea soup was sold hot in the streets of Greece. Roman literature refers to peas as a poor man's food although the recipes they left us prove they were relished by wealthy epicures.

Like other pulses in the legume family (Chapter Six) — peas, beans, lentils, and other plants that bear their seeds in pods that split open when ripe — peas can be enjoyed fresh or dried.

Fresh peas are a clear, bright green. When the pods turn hard, it indicates peas that are overmature and on the way to becoming completely dried. At that point, they are good keepers. Generally, try to buy two and a half times the weight of shelled peas.

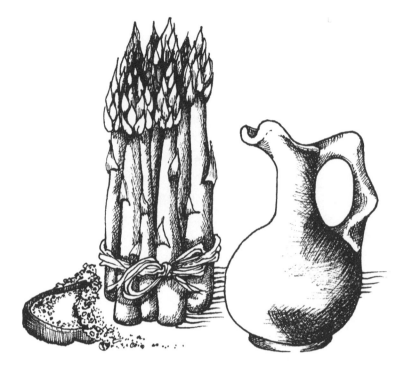

ASPARAGUS AARON

2 tbsp. butter
1 lb. asparagus, cleaned and cut into 1 inch pieces
¾ cup heavy cream
  salt and freshly ground black pepper to taste
¾ cup grated Parmesan cheese
½ cup bread crumbs

Preheat oven to 350°.

Melt the butter in a skillet and quickly sauté the asparagus for 2-3 minutes. They should be bright green and crisp. Transfer to a bake and serve casserole. Pour the cream over the asparagus and add salt and pepper. Sprinkle the cheese over the top. Sprinkle bread crumbs over that. Place casserole in a pan of hot water and bake until fairly set, about 30-35 minutes.

GREEN BEANS JOSHUA

2 lbs. fresh (or frozen) green beans
1 medium onion
3 tbsp. butter
   dash salt
¼ tbsp. each finely chopped parsley, chives, and basil

Steam the green beans in a small amount of boiling water until they are tender. In the meantime, chop the onion finely and put in saucepan with the melted butter. Cook until the onion is golden brown.

When the beans are done, drain well and add to the butter and onion mixture. Sauté a few minutes, shaking the pan so the onion mixes with the beans. Add a dash of salt and sprinkle with the finely chopped herbs.

APPLE AND EVE BEETS

 3 cups sliced cooked beets
 3 cups thinly sliced tart apples
 ½ cup apple juice
 ½ cup thinly sliced onions
 ½ tsp. salt
 1 tbsp. honey
 2 tbsp. lemon juice
 2 tsp. cinnamon
 3 tbsp. butter

Preheat oven to 325°.

Butter a casserole. Mix all the ingredients, except the butter, into the casserole. Dot with butter over the top. Cover and bake for 45 minutes.

BEETS AND LEEKS IN WINE

1   lb. young whole beets
4   leeks, thinly sliced
½   tsp. cumin
1½ cups vegetable stock
¾   cup white wine

Steam beets in a small amount of water until a fork can easily pierce the beets. Drain. Slice beets. Put them in a saucepan with leeks. Add ground cumin, stock, and wine. Bring to a boil, then simmer until leeks are tender.

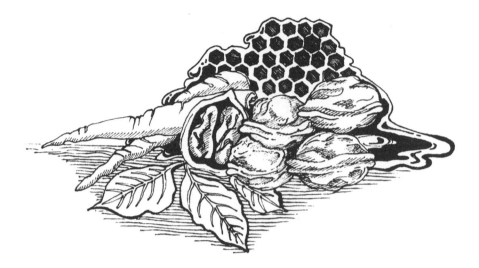

HOLY CARROT

6   medium carrots, cut in diagonal slices, cooked and drained
3   tbsp. butter
¼   cup honey
½   cup chopped walnuts
2   tbsp. prepared mustard
    dash salt
1   tbsp. snipped parsley

Melt butter in a skillet. Stir in honey, walnuts, mustard, and salt. Add cooked carrots. Heat, stirring constantly, until carrots are glazed, about 5 minutes. Sprinkle with parsley.

BEET GREENS OCTAVIUS

¾ cup raisins
5 bunches beet greens (about 3 lbs.)
1 small bunch fresh mint
2 medium red onions
3 cloves garlic
¼ bay leaf
½ cup olive oil
   salt and pepper to taste

Cover raisins with boiling water, set aside for 15 minutes. Wash the beet greens, discard the stems. Cut into fine strips. Do the same to the mint leaves. Peel onions and garlic and mince. Sauté onions, garlic, and bay leaf in ¼ cup olive oil about five minutes. Add beet leaves and raisins and cook covered an additional five minutes. Add the mint, season with salt and pepper, and serve.

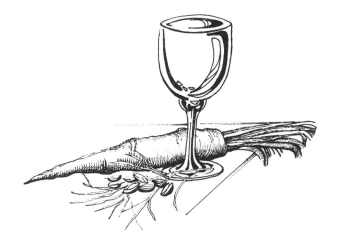

CARROTS JULIUS

8 medium carrots
½ cup white wine
½ cup vegetable stock
2 tsp. olive oil
   dash ground cumin
   salt and pepper to taste

Thinly slice carrots lengthwise. In skillet, put together mixture of wine, stock, and olive oil. Add sliced carrots and sauté until tender. Season with ground cumin and salt and pepper to taste.

CARROT ROLLS

Dough:

1   pkg. dry yeast
1   cup warm water
1   tsp. honey
3   cups whole wheat flour
1   tsp. salt
1   tbsp. olive oil

Dissolve the yeast and honey in warm water. Make a well of the flour and pour yeast mixture into the flour on a clean smooth surface or mix in food processor, adding flour and salt, mixing until it combines into a dough ball. Knead until smooth and soft, adding more flour if necessary. Place in a large, oiled bowl, cover, and let rise in a warm place until double in size. Punch the dough down, cut off one-half, and roll out on a floured board. This dough can be frozen, then thawed whenever needed, and stuffed with other vegetables, spread with pesto, or, sometimes when you're not eating according to the Book, made into a pizza dough. Be sure to let it rise in a warm place before using.

To assemble the carrot rolls:

2-3 large fresh carrots (the thicker ones have more flavor),
      scrubbed and grated
1   small chopped onion
1   cup shredded Cheddar (or any similar hard) cheese
      olive oil
      dash salt
      dash nutmeg
1   beaten egg mixed with 1 tbsp. water

Preheat oven to 350º.

Combine the shredded carrots with the chopped onion and cheese. Roll the dough into a thin rectangle and place on a greased cookie sheet. Spread the carrot mixture over the dough. Drizzle a little olive oil on top, season with salt and a dash of nutmeg, then roll the dough like a jelly roll, rolling the longer sides toward each other, making sure the seam ends up on the bottom.

With a fork, punch a few holes in the roll, then brush it with the beaten egg. Bake for 40 minutes. Slice and serve hot, warm, or cold.

CARROTS AND TURNIPS ZEBULUN

5 large carrots
6 medium size turnips
¼ cup honey (orange blossom if available)
½ cup olive oil
   salt and pepper to taste
¼ cup fresh chopped parsley and mint

Preheat oven to 400°.

Scrub and trim carrots and turnips. Slice carrots diagonally, slice turnips in strips.

Toss vegetables in a large bowl with the olive oil and honey. Season with salt and pepper. Spread in a roasting pan and roast uncovered for 30-45 minutes. Stir and toss once or twice. Remove from oven, sprinkle herbs over vegetables, and serve.

If you haven't done so already, try roasted garlic cloves. They turn out to be creamy, soft, and mild — nothing like you'd imagine.

ROASTED GARLIC

6   heads of garlic
½   cup olive oil (approximately)
    salt and pepper to taste
¼   cup minced rosemary

Preheat the oven to 350°.

Partially remove loose garlic skin. Don't peel, just brush away the papery skins. Use a pastry brush to slaver olive oil over the garlic heads (*heads*, not cloves, one for each person served). Arrange the garlic in an ovenproof dish, pointed ends up. Add enough stock or water to roughly cover one-quarter of an inch of the garlic. Sprinkle with salt, pepper, and rosemary and cover tightly with foil. Bake 35-40 minutes or longer until soft. Keep checking to make sure all the liquid hasn't cooked away. Add a little more oil and continue roasting, uncovered, another five or ten minutes.

To eat, remove the outer skin of the bulb, slit the clove with a knife, and ease out the pulp. Garlic is wonderful with grilled food, hearty bread, in sauces, or mashed and added to soups or other vegetables, especially mashed potatoes, which we shouldn't mention because spuds were a New World crop, unknown to Bible folks.

ROASTED GARLIC II

Preheat oven to 300°.

Follow above recipe, omitting rosemary if desired. Place the prepared garlic flat side down on a double layer of heavy-duty foil, drizzle the olive oil over the garlic, season with salt and pepper, adding basil or oregano lightly, then wrap the foil tightly around the packet.

Roast for 30 minutes or until it feels soft when pressed. Serve warm or at room temperature.

PHARAOH'S ONIONS

  3 tbsp. butter
      salt and pepper to taste
  ¼ cup white wine
10-12 small onions, cooked and drained
  ¼ cup grated Parmesan cheese

Melt butter in saucepan. Stir in seasonings and wine. Add onions and sauté quickly (about 5 minutes), stirring a few times. Turn into serving dish and sprinkle with cheese.

FABULLUS PEAS

2 lbs. freshly shelled or frozen peas
1 lettuce heart, finely shredded
1 bunch chopped spring onions
   salt and pepper to taste
¾ cup boiling water
3 tbsp. butter
2 tsp. flour
½ tsp. ginger

Put the peas, lettuce, spring onions, and salt into a saucepan. Pour the boiling water over, cover, and cook gently for about 10 minutes or until the peas are tender. This will depend on whether they are frozen or fresh and whether they are *petite pois* or larger.

Cream a little of the butter with the flour and add the mixture a spoonful at a time to the peas, stirring well between each addition. Cook over low heat an additional 2 minutes. Stir in the remainder of the butter, taste, and adjust the seasoning.

PEAS 'N' CHEESE

3   cups cooked peas
1   tsp. minced fresh mint
¾   cup grated Cheddar cheese
3   eggs
1½ cups milk or cream
     salt and pepper to taste

Preheat oven to 350°.

Put the cooked peas in a buttered 1½ quart baking dish. Sprinkle with the mint and the cheese. Beat the eggs in a bowl. Stir in the milk or cream and a dash of salt and pepper. Add to the cheese and peas mixture.

Place the baking dish in a shallow pan with hot water halfway up the sides. Bake for 45-60 minutes or until the custard is set.

TURNIPS SHEBA

  2 lbs. white turnips
12 whole wheat bread slices
1⅛ cups Swiss cheese, shredded
⅜ cup chopped green onions
  2 cloves crushed garlic
  4 eggs, slightly beaten
  2 cups milk
½ cup yogurt
  1 tsp. ground dried or 2 tbsp. fresh basil minced
     salt and pepper to taste
  1 tbsp. finely chopped parsley

If the turnips are small and young, scrub them. If older, they must be peeled. Slice. Cook in boiling water 8-10 minutes.

Butter a large pan or baking dish. Place 6 slices of the bread in the bottom of pan. Spread the cooked, sliced turnips over the bread. Sprinkle with ½ cup of the cheese, the garlic, and the green onions. Top with remaining bread slices.

Combine eggs, milk, yogurt, and basil in small bowl; mix well. Pour the egg mixture over the bread; press so the bread is covered with the liquid.

Cover and refrigerate 30 minutes or longer.

Preheat oven to 350°. Uncover and top with the remaining cheese, dash of salt and pepper, and the chopped parsley.

Bake 30-35 minutes. It is done when a knife inserted near the center comes out clean. Let stand 10-15 minutes before serving.

MIXED VEGETABLES UZZIAH

1   cup wine
2   cups olive oil
½   cup lemon juice
½   cup water
2   cloves garlic, crushed
3   sprigs parsley, chopped
     additional lemon juice
     salt to taste
     dash of thyme, coriander, and fennel

Combine the wine, olive oil, lemon juice, water, and crushed garlic in a stainless steel or enamel saucepan. Cook over a low heat until reduced by one-third.

Clean and prepare the following:

1   lb. julienned carrots
2   stalks celery, sliced
½   lb. green beans
2   leeks, sliced
1   medium onion, diced
½   lb. cubed feta cheese
½   lb. green olives

Squeeze lemon juice over the cut vegetables.

Preheat the oven to 325°.

Place the seasoned liquid over the heat once more and again bring to a boil. Simmer the onions and leeks in the liquid and cook to just before the tender stage. Remove and place in a casserole. Continue with the green beans and carrots. Cook until they're tender. Remove to the casserole.

Stir gently to combine. Strain the liquid over the vegetables, add olives, dot with the feta cheese. Bake 15-20 minutes until the mixture is heated through.

Take the rest of the day off.

Chapter Four

SALADS

Lettuce, endive, chicory, and dandelion are all mentioned in the Talmud as bitter herbs to be eaten during Passover.

 The fourteenth day of the second month at even they shall keep it, and eat it with unleavened bread and bitter herbs.
(Numbers 9:11)

Lettuce (Lactuca sativa) undoubtedly grew wild all over East Asia before being brought into cultivation. It was eaten in ancient Egypt; its seeds have been found in tombs. The fertility god, Min, had lettuce offered to him — its milk was thought to have aphrodisiac qualities. The Assyrians concurred and lettuce grew in King Merodach-Baladan's garden. Both Hippocrates and Aristotle mention lettuce, which was apparently an all-inclusive term that took in chicory, endive, chervil, and purslane. Both dandelion and watercress were also prized, but the variety with the longest pedigree is romaine. It is sometimes called cos, named for an island off the coast of Greece. Now we use it to make Caesar salad as did the original Caesars.

It's interesting that purslane, considered a weed growing wild for generations, is once again touted as a vitamin-rich addition to the salad garden.

Almost any non-toxic green leaf with a palatable flavor qualifies as a salad green, and it's difficult to determine the difference between salad greens and herbs, but lettuce has been prized from earliest times, mostly in its leafy (rather than head lettuce) forms. The Roman Theophrastus lists four kinds of lettuce, all loose leaf varieties — heading lettuce was developed much later.

Lettuce was eaten as a salad with a dressing, just as we do today, although Apicius left us a recipe for a purée of lettuce leaves and onions.

Today, as any garden catalog points out, lettuce is described as a hardy, annual herb with numerous varieties and strains. It should be quickly grown in fertile, well-drained soil with a steady supply of moisture.

To create a great salad, use a variety of mixed greens — the deepest darkest leaves like romaine are the most healthful. Aim for various colors, textures, and flavors. A salad spinner is invaluable for washing off all that fertile garden loam.

Tear the leaves into bite-sized pieces. Add curly endive, chives, Italian parsley, purslane, if you can find it, and mint leaves. Also savory, rue, green onions, thyme — even cat mint, also known as catnip, exciting to felines the world over.

> *Thou shalt have olive trees throughout all thy coasts . . .*
> (Deuteronomy 28:40)

There's no argument about olives being mentioned in the Bible. The olive tree (Olea europaea) was the most important tree cultivated in early times.

Over five thousand years ago groves of olive trees flourished amid the rocks and poor soil on the mountain slopes of Galilee, Samaria, and Judea, crowned by the Mount of Olives in the ancient kingdom of Jerusalem. The olive branch has symbolized peace and hope ever since the dove came back to Noah with a freshly plucked leaf in its bill.

> *Blessed is every one that feareth the Lord; that walketh in his ways. For thou shalt eat the labour of thine hands: happy shalt thou be, and it shall be well with thee. Thy wife shall be as a fruitful vine by the sides of thine house: thy children like olive plants round about thy table.*
> (Psalms 128:1-3)

One tree could supply a whole family with oil since a full-sized tree might yield a half ton of oil each year. No wonder it was a symbol of prosperity. Olive oil provided food, medicine, and fuel for lamps. It was used in holy ointments of kings and priests; for anointing the sick; as a solvent of various spices, incenses, and aromatics used in the making of perfumes and cosmetics. The richly grained wood of the olive tree was carved into ornaments and all kinds of household utensils.

There are 400 species. The tree often grows wild and although it's a slow starter, it lasts into great age and bears fruit even after the trunk is hollow. Some olive groves in Israel are thought to be more than a thousand years old.

Leaves are a soft gray-green below and blue-green above and are willow-like. Smooth gray trunks and branches become gnarled in maturity. Trees eventually reach 25-30 feet high and spread as wide. Clusters of small white flowers appear between April and June and are shed soon after pollination when the flowers have produced tiny berries the size of pinheads. These subsequently fill out with flesh and develop a stone.

Green olives are unripened fruit, about an inch long. In the harvest time from August to November, long poles are used to beat the olives from the branches.

The ripe black olives, which contain more oil than green ones, are gathered into baskets, then crushed by a large stone wheel. The oil runs off through a spout.

In olden times, small quantities were pounded separately in a mortar to prepare the oil for the lamps of the Temple.

> *And thou shalt command the children of Israel, that they bring thee pure oil olive beaten for the light, to cause the lamp to burn always.*
>
> (Exodus 27:20)

Then as now, bread was dipped in olive oil and the oil used daily in cooking. It was also valuable as a dressing to soften wounds, as a kind of suntan lotion, for liniments and soap. The ancient Greeks massaged it into athletes' bodies before they exercised. They mixed it with honey to preserve fabrics. Sophocles called it "the tree that stands unequaled."

In Crete, where olive oil was considered the king's treasure, it was stored in vast quantities in pottery jars in the storerooms of the palace at Knossos.

Once the olive reached Italy, its value was soon appreciated. Aside from the refined appetites of the gourmets, it fed the poor. Cato reports that bread, wine, salt, and olives were the staple diet of the peasants and working class.

Olive oil is still prepared in the old way. The olives are covered with hot water, crushed, then held in large vats with a drain at the bottom. The oil floats to the surface. Finally, the water is drained from the bottom and the pure oil remains at the top.

Gethsemane, at the foot of the Mount of Olives where Jesus spent the night before his crucifixion, is the garden where the oil flowed exuberantly, surrounded by the picturesque groves.

Considered completely digestible because of its high content of oleic acid, the use of olive oil increases the absorption of fat-soluble vitamins A, D, E, and K.

In the cholesterol controversy, some authorities say people with heart trouble should eschew *all* fat including the so-called good canola and olive oils. Others point out that substituting olive oil for saturated fats helps to lower the risk of coronary artery disease by raising the level of good lipoproteins that prevent cholesterol deposits from adhering to artery walls.

Which advice to heed? It appears to change almost hourly, so the best plan seems to be to stay informed, keep your ears open, read, and ask questions.

If you decide to go with olive oil, a few pointers. Oil is considered extra-virgin if it has less than one percent acidity, is cold pressed, and perfect in flavor and aroma.

Are we the only ones who think that extra virgin is funny? Isn't the word *virgin* an absolute, a state, not a stage—used to describe purity—pure? It's like saying something is more or less unique which the dictionary defines as being the only one of its kind. How then could something be more?

If the acid level is between one and three percent, it is classified as virgin and the taste is sharper. If it does not meet those exacting standards, refined olive oil is marketed that may be blended with 5-10 percent virgin olive oil to improve its flavor and color and then sold as pure.

Use extra-virgin oil in salads or other uncooked dishes; lesser quality oils in recipes where the flavor is dominated by other ingredients. Cold pressed oils made by hydraulic pressure are always best. Like butter, olive oil should be refrigerated to prevent rancidity once it is opened. When the oil solidifies due to cold, either remember to remove it from the refrigerator half an hour before using or hold the sealed bottle under hot tap water.

The radish (Raphanus sativus) is another annual herb grown for its crisp-fleshed roots. Not mentioned by this name in the Bible, it is nevertheless of great antiquity. Radish seed contains oil which was used before olives were grown. The green prickly leaves were eaten, too. When cooked as greens, the prickles disappear.

The secret to growing crisp, mild radishes of the best quality is to bring them along rapidly and harvest when they're small if you choose to eat them raw. The ancients grew them quite large, however, and cooked them along with their green leaves. Steamed, they taste like turnips. This may or may not be an inducement to trying them.

Apicius advises that we serve radishes with pepper sauce made by grinding pepper and mixing with fish-pickle sauce the Romans called *li-quamen*. Of course, he thought it was a good idea to serve *everything* with fish-pickle sauce except strawberry shortcake!

APICIUS' FISH-PICKLE SAUCE

3   oz. drained canned tuna or salmon, sardines, or anchovies
1   tbsp. white wine
1   tbsp. vinegar
1   tbsp. olive oil
1   clove of crushed garlic
¼   tsp. pepper
2   tsp. parsley
¼   tsp. ground rosemary
¼   tsp. sage
1   finely chopped mint leaf
    pinch of basil

In a food processor, thoroughly pulse-chop to combine all ingredients. Store in a glass jar for up to three weeks in refrigerator. Use as a salad dressing.

BASIC MAYONNAISE

Before you start, a few tips. All ingredients must be at room temperature — eggs, olive oil, lemon juice, as well as the blender. Take things out of the refrigerator at least half an hour before. Rinse the blender with hot water and dry it just before you begin. Don't try to make mayonnaise during a thunderstorm or if it's seriously threatening — the mayo won't come together.

If it *does* curdle and refuses to thicken, take another egg out of the refrigerator and warm it in a bowl of warm water. Remove it from the bowl, rinse the bowl with hot water, dry it, separate the egg yolk from the white, and place the yolk in the bowl. Whisk and very, very slowly add a tiny bit of the curdled dressing, whisking and slowly adding more as the mixture thickens.

Another good way, if you're patient, is to pour the curdled mixture into a bowl, wash the blender, dry it, put the new egg yolk in, and very slowly return the curdled concoction. Sounds complicated, but it isn't. And it works. Now, back to basic mayonnaise:

2   eggs
1   tsp. mustard powder
1   tsp. salt
3   tbsp. lemon juice
     olive oil

Break the eggs into the blender. Cover and blend on the slowest speed as you add the mustard, salt, and ¼ C olive oil. With blender still running, take off the cover and slowly add ½ C olive oil, then 3 tbsp. lemon juice. Add another ½ C olive oil. You will have to stop and stir down the sides with a rubber spatula. When you continue, if all the oil has been used and the blades can still turn, drip in more oil until it absolutely won't take any more.

This mayonnaise is excellent on leftover fish. It makes a superb chicken salad. Try chopped walnuts and grapes in the chicken salad, too.

As a variation on the basic mayonnaise recipe, blend in parsley, shallots, and/or green onion tops for a green dressing. Or blend in three or four garlic cloves, grated orange peel, capers, freshly ground pepper, and a pinch of salt and serve over poached fish and/or vegetables. Now you can call it aïoli, famed as the butter of Provence.

CHICKEN SALAD

Boil chicken, following recipe in Chapter 7 for Chicken Pilaf. Dice cooked, cooled chicken. Mix with homemade mayonnaise, halved grapes (or black olives), chopped walnuts, and/or pine nuts. Season with sage, basil, and salt. Taste and adjust seasonings.

HEAVEN ON EARTH SALAD DRESSING

½ cup extra-virgin mild tasting olive oil
⅓ cup fresh lemon juice
2 large cloves of crushed garlic
½ tsp. seasoned salt (Vege-Sal or Spike)
    dash ground pepper
1 tsp. mustard powder
    approximately ½ tsp. each fresh or dried oregano, basil,
    tarragon leaves, and mint

Combine in 8 oz. glass jar. Screw lid on tightly. Shake. Taste — it may need more lemon juice, salt, or garlic — and adjust seasonings.

Before storing in refrigerator, place jar in the center of a square of paper towel, bring up the ends, and slip a rubber band around the jar.

This is a great salad dressing. Your kids will invite you to their dinner parties if you promise to bring some along. Remember to take it out of the refrigerator half an hour before preparing the salad. Shake well before opening. For each individual salad, try 3 tablespoonfuls. Toss.

His branches shall spread, and his beauty shall be as the olive tree, and his smell as Lebanon.

(Hosea 14:6)

SALAD DRESSING HOSEA

½ cup olive oil
3 tbsp. lemon juice
1 tsp. salt
1 tbsp. capers
1 tbsp. minced parsley

Combine all ingredients in a jar. Shake well.

This dressing is good over a typical Greek salad with feta cheese and fresh raw vegetables.

It can also be used as a marinade for chicken, fish, or cooked vegetables.

HONEY NUT DRESSING

1 cup yogurt
1 tbsp. fresh lemon juice
3 tbsp. honey
¼ cup walnuts (or pine nuts), toasted and chopped
  few mint leaves, chopped
½ tsp. cinnamon

Blend lemon juice and honey into yogurt, adding more of either to reach desired taste and consistency. Stir in nuts and mint leaves immediately before serving.

Serve over fruit salad or use as a dip for raw vegetables and fruit. Try it with carrots, celery, or chunks of apples and pears, sections of oranges or spooned over melon.

SERAPHIC PARK

4 cups seedless grapes
2 tbsp. minced spring onions
2 tbsp. chopped parsley
2 tbsp. chopped mint
½ cup pine nuts, lightly toasted
mixed romaine and loose leaf lettuce

Cut grapes in half. Toss with herbs and nuts. Make beds of lettuce on six serving plates and place a mound of grapes on each. Drizzle with Heaven on Earth dressing.

PESTO ROMANO

1 cup chopped fresh basil
3 garlic cloves, minced
½ cup grated Parmesan cheese
½ cup walnuts or pine nuts, chopped
1 cup olive oil (approximately)
   salt and pepper to taste

Add chopped basil leaves to food processor or blender until pulverized. Add chopped nuts, minced garlic, and cheese. While machine is running, slowly pour in a thin stream of oil. Continue blending until smooth. Stop often to scrape sides of blender, adding more oil if needed. Don't be afraid to add more garlic, cheese, or nuts until it tastes Lucullan. This is not a liquid sauce — it's more of a paste.

Use it over chicken or cooked lentils. The sauce may be frozen.

JULIUTH ICTHUS SALAD

¾ cup olive oil
4 cloves of garlic
4 tbsp. lemon juice, more or less, to taste
   dash of salt
4 anchovy fillets
2 heads romaine lettuce
2½ cups croutons*
½ cup Parmesan cheese, freshly grated

*Croutons: Use up slightly stale bread. Remove the crusts, then cut slices of bread into cubes. Sauté in hot butter or olive oil. Add minced clove of garlic when all sides of the bread have browned, taking care not to let the garlic burn.

In a blender, combine the olive oil and garlic. Blend until creamy. Add the lemon juice and salt. Pour the dressing into a large salad bowl. Add the anchovies and mash into the dressing.

Wash and dry the lettuce leaves, discarding any that are blemished. Tear into bite-sized pieces. Add to the salad bowl and toss until the leaves are coated. Add the croutons and toss lightly. Just before serving, add the cheese.

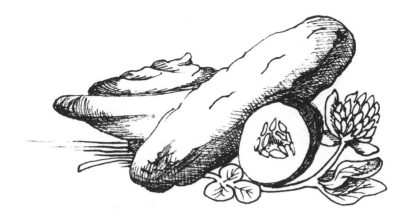

RICH AS CROESUS' MINT

2¼ large cucumbers
    salt and pepper to taste
1½ cups plain yogurt
1½ tsp. lemon juice
 ½ tsp. honey
 3 tbsp. fresh mint, chopped
1½ tbsp. green onion, minced

Peel, seed, and chop cucumbers only if they're waxed. If homegrown, young and tender-skinned, just wash, dry, and chop. Sprinkle with salt and allow to drain for half an hour.

Line a sieve with a coffee filter or cheesecloth. Pour yogurt in and allow to drain for half an hour. In a glass or pottery serving bowl, combine yogurt with remaining ingredients. Stir in cucumber. Serve at once.

MORE CUCUMBER SALAD

1½ cups lowfat yogurt
 6 tbsp. scallions, chopped
½ tsp. dill (dried)
½ tsp. salt
½ tsp. mustard powder
 3 cucumbers, sliced
    dill weed sprigs, for garnish

In small bowl, combine the yogurt, scallions, dill, salt, and mustard powder. Blend. Add thinly sliced cucumbers and mix well to coat with dressing. Place 2 or 3 dill sprigs on top. Cover tightly and refrigerate for one hour. Before serving, remove dill.

SALAD JOSHUA

¼ cup pine nuts
1 head of leaf lettuce, washed and dried
4 oz. feta cheese, crumbled
1 cup seedless grapes, halved
pinch salt
3 tbsp. lemon juice
½ cup olive oil

Brown pine nuts over medium heat, stirring continuously, about 2 minutes. Set aside.

Tear lettuce into bite-sized pieces. Place in bowl and add pine nuts, feta cheese, and grapes. In a separate small bowl dissolve salt in lemon juice. Whisk in olive oil and taste for seasoning. Drizzle over salad, toss, and serve.

LOTTA LENTILS

¼ cup fresh lemon juice
⅔ cup olive oil
2 tsp. mixed herbs: mint, basil, and thyme
1 clove garlic, mashed
2 cups dried lentils
½ cup finely diced celery

Whisk together lemon juice and olive oil. Beat in herbs and garlic.

Wash lentils and boil in a quart of water until tender, about 30 minutes. Drain. While warm, toss with lemon dressing. Cool to room temperature. Add celery. Serve immediately or chill and serve cold.

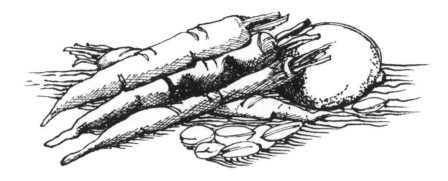

CARROT SUNSHINE SALAD

2 lbs. carrots, scrubbed, grated, and thinly sliced
4 oranges, peeled, sectioned, and chopped
½ lb. grapes
   juice of 1 lemon
2 tbsp. mint, chopped
1 cup raisins
½ cup toasted pistachios or pine nuts
¾ cup mayonnaise

Toss all the ingredients together in a large bowl. Serve cold.

OLIVE CITRUS SALAD

3   oranges, peeled, sectioned, and chopped
    lettuce
2   scallions, sliced
½   cup pitted black olives
¼   cup garlic mayonnaise
    juice of ½ lemon
½   tsp. coriander

Wash and tear lettuce into bite-sized pieces, enough to line six salad plates. Toss the oranges, scallions, and olives together. In a separate small bowl, combine the mayonnaise, lemon juice, and coriander. Add to orange mixture. Toss together, then divide among the salad plates.

ROAMIN' SALAD

1 head romaine lettuce
1 clove of garlic, peeled and cut in half
4 tbsp. lemon juice
5 tbsp. olive oil
1 tsp. powdered mustard
1 egg yolk
1 orange, peeled, seeded, and sliced
1 cup croutons
   grated cheese
   dash of pepper, freshly ground

Tear washed lettuce leaves into bite-sized pieces. Rub the garlic halves around the inside of a large wooden salad bowl and discard the garlic.

Combine the lemon juice, olive oil, and powdered mustard in a large salad bowl. Stir in the egg yolk. Add the lettuce, orange, croutons, and grated cheese. Toss, then add the ground pepper and additional cheese to taste.

KIDNEY BEAN SALAD

6 cups cooked red kidney beans
½ cup artichoke hearts, diced
2 tbsp. green onions, chopped
2 cloves of garlic, chopped
1 tbsp. chopped parsley
2 tbsp. chopped fresh basil
   juice of 1 lemon (or 2 tbsp. wine vinegar)
6 tbsp. olive oil
   salt and ground pepper to taste
   lettuce leaves

Drain the beans and put in a large mixing bowl. Add the rest of the ingredients (except for the lettuce) and toss gently to coat the beans. Taste, adjusting the seasonings. Line a salad bowl with lettuce leaves and arrange the beans on top. Garnish with sprigs of parsley.

Chapter Five

DAIRY

Because milk was transported in skin bags slung over a donkey's back for thousands of years, it was inevitable that butter would be produced. All that sloshing. The one dispensable element was the donkey!

The words of his mouth were smoother than butter, but war was in his heart: his words were softer than oil, yet were they drawn swords.

(Psalms 55:21)

Mankind has enjoyed butter for more than five thousand years. It was first used as a medicine, only later as a spread. Butter was thought of then as a common food, enjoyed by shepherds, but olive oil was preferred for cooking.

Butter of kine, and milk of sheep, with fat of lambs, and rams of the breed of Bashan, and goats, with the fat of kidneys of wheat; and thou didst drink the pure blood of the grape.

(Deuteronomy 32:14)

Farm-fresh butter, made with sweet cream, is close to yellow in color in summer, reflecting the higher amounts of carotene the cows ingest. It is, naturally, a much lighter color in winter when they've eaten dry fodder.

Today, butter is less wholesome than it used to be with additives taking the place of freshness, another case of unnatural ingredients supplanting what was natural and pure. Salt is added to retard the growth of yeast and molds and extend shelf life. Coal tar dyes are used to force the summer-yellow color.

Whenever possible unsalted, first quality sweet cream butter is preferred.

> *He asked water, and she gave him milk; she brought forth*
> *butter in a lordly dish.*
>
> (Judges 5:25)

If you're going to serve it in a lordly dish, shouldn't the butter be the very best?

> *Hast thou not poured me out as milk, and curdled me like*
> *cheese?*
>
> (Job 10:10)

Cheese was probably discovered in the same accidental way as butter. Milk and other liquids were carried in bags made from the skins of goats' or sheeps' stomachs. Since the stomachs of young mammals living on milk contain a digestive substance called rennet, and since even today cheese is made from milk curdled with rennet added, it's obvious how the first cottage cheese came about.

The Bible describes three kinds of dairy products, which roughly correspond to soft cheese, hard cheese, and yogurt. The original King James Version translates all three as "butter," but later translations use the word "curds," which may be more accurate.

> *And it shall come to pass, for the abundance of milk that*
> *they shall give he shall eat butter: for butter and honey*
> *shall every one eat that is left in the land.*
>
> (Isaiah 7:22)

So when there was an abundance of milk, the household soon turned it into cheese. An Egyptian tomb of five thousand years ago was discovered with a lady's remains. Next to her was a jar of some kind of cheese, probably made from camel's milk and no doubt intended to nourish her in the afterworld.

Clay tablets have been found in the city of Ur dating back to 2000 B.C. that refer to cheese. The Greeks were very fond of cheese and have handed down some terrific recipes. The Romans refined cheese making even further and relished a variety of locally grown as well as imported cheeses.

If a bird's nest chance to be before thee in the way in any tree, or on the ground, whether they be young ones, or eggs, and the dam sitting upon the young, or upon the eggs, thou shalt not take the dam with the young:

(Deuteronomy 22:6)

An egg is nature's flawless package. It carries life from one generation to another and contains everything necessary for the creation of that new life, whether moth, ostrich, or human being.

"I think if required on pain of death to name the most perfect thing in the universe, I should risk my fate on a bird's egg," wrote naturalist T.W. Higginson over a hundred years ago.

But ever since man first crawled out of the primordial ooze, he has lifted some kind of egg from a bird's nest and consumed its contents raw, steamed, boiled, poached, scrambled, baked, or fried. Archeologists have found bird bones, eggshells, and drawings of poultry in cave ruins. In ancient times, eggs were thought to be an aphrodisiac, the symbol of life, regeneration, and spring.

And my hand hath found as a nest the riches of the people: and as one gathereth eggs that are left, have I gathered all the earth; and there was none that moved the wing, or opened the mouth, or peeped.

(Isaiah 10:14)

The concept that a secret life was developing inside a fragile shell unattended by any external influence inspired men and women with a deep religious respect. The sacred egg was venerated by the ancient Egyptians. Their priests refused to eat them, not wanting to offend the creative powers. There was even a time when the cock was worshipped as a god and admired for his strength and courage for heralding each dawn, while the hen, presumably the very symbol of fertility, kept on modestly clucking along, laying an egg a day.

In Greek tombs circa 1250 B.C., experts have testified to the presence of goose eggshells.

A seal from the Sixth Century B.C. Palestine depicts a rooster, so chicken eggs were eaten then along with duck, goose, partridge, ostrich, and wild bird eggs. Some scholars believe the chicken was unknown until after 1000 B.C. when it was introduced from Persia.

As the partridge sitteth on eggs, and hatcheth them not; so he that getteth riches, and not by right, shall leave them in the midst of his days, and at his end shall be a fool.

(Jeremiah 17:11)

Our own chickens may have descended from the red jungle fowl (Gallus gallus) of Asia, a much smaller breed than we know today, and there is evidence that it was valued more for the rooster's fighting abilities than for the egg-laying talents of its fairer feathered hens.

The wild jungle fowl brought forth 25-50 eggs a year while current domestic breeds produce up to 300, and each hen lays eggs for most of her life. Hens allowed to range freely lay a clutch of eggs, mostly in the warmer months when days are longer. Then they sit on them until they hatch, but on modern poultry farms artificial light and heat are controlled. The eggs roll away as soon as they're laid, and the hens' broody maternal instincts are frustrated, inspiring the hens to lay continuously.

Without benefit of electric light Our Mothers kept geese and ducks over five thousand years ago. When chickens became domesticated, they were raised by the Egyptians, Greeks, and Romans, brought to Western Europe and Britain, then to the New World by Spanish explorers around 100 A.D.

In ancient Jewish rituals both rooster and hen were carried in the bridal procession. The Greeks placed eggs on the altars of their temples as sacrifices to the deities while the Romans brought caged chickens along to battle to serve as feathered oracles. If the birds ate the grain put before them, it was a good omen and that day's battle could proceed. Otherwise, the carnage would be postponed. Naturally, some generals figured out how to beat the system by starving the chickens before requesting that day's permission to fight.

Today we eat mostly chicken eggs. Found all over the world, from the meanest villages to the highest citadels of gourmet cuisine, we face them at breakfast day after day, taking them as much for granted as the bread we dip in the runny yolk. Yet there are somewhere around 8600 different kinds of birds, and every one of them taps out of its eggshell to snag its first glimpse of the wide world.

Long before the Christian era, eggs were colored, blessed, and exchanged as part of the rites of spring to welcome the sun's awakening from the long winter's sleep.

Ester or *Eostre,* originally the name of the pagan vernal festival, became the paschal holiday of the Resurrection of Jesus held on the Sunday following the full moon on or after the spring equinox.

In Europe, giving eggs at Easter dates back to the Middle Ages. At that time, eating eggs was forbidden during the forty days of Lent. The hens continued to lay, of course, and by Easter there was a surplus. Starting on Good Friday children, students, and choir boys sang hymns at church, then paraded through town collecting eggs from house to house. Afterwards, they enjoyed huge omelets.

The rabbit was another symbol of fertility, so it was a natural hop to the Easter bunny leaving colored eggs in children's baskets.

By the eighteenth century, ordinary people continued to dye and decorate hens' eggs. They also created eggs of glass, papier-mâché, or porcelain. The aristocracy in Paris, Berlin, and St. Petersburg commissioned elaborate gold, silver, and enamel eggs set with precious stones. In central Europe, there's a long history of elaborately decorated Easter eggs. Yugoslavian Easter eggs bear the initials XV for Christ is Risen, a traditional Easter greeting. In Russia they celebrated the Resurrection and the beginning of spring by exchanging three kisses and an egg, which are most often dyed and decorated—the egg, not the kisses.

Easter eggs have special names in various languages: *pissankis* in Russian; *pisankis* in Polish; *kraslices* in Czech; *paquelets* in France; and *cocognes* in Belgium; with each group having its own specific design and color combinations.

In 1884 when Tsar Alexander III wished to give his Danish-born wife a very special Easter present, Peter Carl Fabergé, goldsmith and jeweler to the Russian Imperial Court, presented what looked like an ordinary hen's egg fashioned from opaque white enamel over gold. Inside was the surprise — a golden yolk. Within the yolk was a hen made of gold with two cabochon ruby eyes. The hen displayed a model of the Imperial Crown with a tiny ruby egg nestled inside the crown.

This may be what Mark Twain had in mind when he wrote: "Put all your eggs in one basket and WATCH THAT BASKET!"

Eggs, of course, supply complete protein and amino acids necessary to health. They are an excellent source of unsaturated fatty acids, iron, phosphorus, trace minerals, vitamins A, E, K, B complex, and vitamin D.

On the other hand there is the "high-cholesterol-contributes-to-heart-disease" controversy. The final decision is up to you and the best medical advice you can come up with.

Eggs are rich in lecithin, which some believe helps the body utilize

cholesterol as long as the eggs are cooked without added fat or in a mini-
mum of vegetable oil instead of bacon drippings, lard, or hydrogenated
(solid) cooking fats. Egg protein is the standard by which all proteins are
judged, second only to mother's milk for human nutrition. An egg yolk
is one of the few foods that naturally contains vitamin D, the sunshine
vitamin.

One way to reduce blood cholesterol is to eat foods of plant origin, a
diet rich in fiber from cereals and legumes, fruits, vegetables, and grains
(and exercise, reduce stress, etc.).

Nutrition experts say the two main influences on blood cholesterol
levels are heredity and saturated fat — not cholesterol consumption. Con-
trary to long-held belief, dietary cholesterol is not strongly implicated in
calculating the risk of coronary artery disease. But we can't ignore the fact
that some people are cholesterol sensitive, and their blood cholesterol levels rise when their dietary consumption of cholesterol increases. Dietary
advice must be individualized. Some of us need to watch our cholesterol
levels more closely than others. Although the whites are both fat and cholesterol free, the yolk of one large egg has 213 milligrams of cholesterol
and five grams of fat, 1.6 of them saturated. As for white vs. brown, Americans seem to prefer white eggs while Brits favor brown. The breed of
chicken determines the color of the shell.

> *Surely the churning of milk bringeth forth butter, and the*
> *wringing of the nose bringeth forth blood: so the forcing*
> *of wrath bringeth forth strife.*
>
> (Proverbs 30:33)

In the west, we tend to think of milk as exclusively from a cow. But
since the goat was probably man's first domesticated animal, goat milk
was far more utilized than cow's milk.

> *And thou shalt have goats' milk enough for thy food, for*
> *the food of thy household, and for the maintenance for*
> *thy maidens.*
>
> (Proverbs 27:27)

Early people also used sheep and camel milk. Today, mankind milks
those as well as reindeer, caribou, water buffalo, yak, llama, and zebu —
not a typo. A zebu is a Tibetan breed of domestic cattle with a large hump

on the shoulders and a prominent dewlap hanging from her neck.

The mineral and protein composition of goat's milk is closer to human's than it is to cow's. Since Hippocrates, goat's milk has been recommended for infants, invalids, orphaned mammals, and those humans allergic to cow's milk. It is naturally homogenized and has more calcium and vitamin A, but a little less protein.

Milk is an excellent complement to vegetable proteins because it contains all the amino acids.

Jewish law prohibited cooking or eating milk and meat at the same meal and that set apart the cuisine of the Hebrews from that of other Middle Eastern groups. However, there was no injunction against taking an animal's milk while its calf stood by bellowing piteously.

When warm milk is infused with healthy lactoacidophilus bacteria, it thickens and becomes yogurt, referred to in the Bible as curds. This is what Abraham served his guests.

> *And he took butter, and milk, and the calf which he had dressed, and set it before them; and he stood by them under the tree, and they did eat.*
>
> (Genesis 18:8)

But was that kosher? The explanation could be that Abraham preceded Moses' Law (set forth in Leviticus), and that could explain why he could serve milk and the dressed calf at the same meal. But what about when David and his people were given yogurt with honey in the following passage:

> *And honey, and butter, and sheep, and cheese of kine, for David, and for the people that were with him, to eat: for they said, The people is hungry, and weary, and thirsty, in the wilderness.*
>
> (II Samuel 17:29)

Perhaps there's a good explanation we haven't come across yet.

Although yogurt is now sold in every market, you might like to try making your own.

BASIC YOGURT

Bring a quart of milk to a full boil.

Set aside to cool to 115°. This feels warm to your wrist.

Stir a little of the milk into 2 tablespoons of plain yogurt, then stir the yogurt mixture into the warm milk. Pour into clean glass jars, cover, and put the jars into a kettle or roasting pan of warm water up to just below the jar tops.

Now it has to rest in a warm place, over a pilot light on top of the stove, inside a barely warm oven, or wrapped in towels for about eight hours until the yogurt is custard-like, at which time it should be refrigerated. The longer it sits after this stage before being cooled, the more tart it becomes. Save two tablespoons for your next starter. (Continue with each batch until the yogurt becomes too thin. That's when you have to buy more commercial yogurt and start again.) Add honey or crushed fruit to eat as is or use in recipes.

Once you have a good supply of fresh yogurt, you can make your own pot cheese by allowing the whey to drain from the yogurt either in a cheesecloth-lined colander or in a paper coffee filter cone over a suitable strainer. Just prop the apparatus so it drains into the sink overnight or into a bowl. Cover the whole thing with plastic and refrigerate.

Flavor with herbs or chopped walnuts and use as a filling for sandwiches and in salads.

These are all good lunches or light dinners. Add a salad, home-baked bread, and a glass of wine and they're positively Biblical!

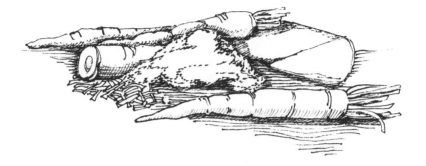

NAOMI'S CARROT-CHEESE BAKE

1½ cups shredded carrots
1 cup julienned leeks
3 tbsp. butter
1 tbsp. flour
1 cup milk
¾ cup grated cheddar cheese
1 tbsp. olive oil
1 clove garlic, peeled and diced
½ cup slivered toasted almonds
 salt and pepper to taste

Preheat oven to 350°.

Steam carrots and leeks for two minutes. Coat the inside of a gratin dish with one tablespoon of butter. Arrange the steamed carrots and leeks on top. Melt two tablespoons of butter in a saucepan over very low heat. Stir in the flour until blended. Slowly add the milk and grated cheese, stirring until smooth and thick. Pour over carrots. In the same skillet, heat the olive oil and garlic, then add the toasted almonds and brown until crisp. Distribute over the carrots and sauce. Salt and pepper to taste. Bake 20 minutes.

It wouldn't take a saint to prepare this simple dish for breakfast, even weekdays, if the whole thing was assembled the night before, refrigerated, then popped into the oven the next morning. Allow a little extra baking time to compensate for the cold ingredients.

SAINTLY EGGS

  2 tbsp. butter
10 oz. Swiss or Gruyère cheese, sliced thin
12 eggs
¾ cup heavy cream
¾ cup Parmesan cheese, grated
     salt and pepper to taste

Preheat oven to 350°.

Butter a shallow casserole dish. Line dish with thin cheese slices. Break the eggs into the casserole dish, keeping them whole. Carefully pour cream over the eggs. Sprinkle with Parmesan cheese and salt and pepper and bake for 15 minutes or until egg whites are set and yolks are still runny. Brown the cheese topping under the broiler for a few minutes.

EZRA'S FRITTERS

6 eggs
2 tbsp. water
¼ cup chopped mint
¼ cup minced parsley
½ cup minced green onions (or chopped white onion)
2 tsp. flour
   dash nutmeg
   salt and pepper to taste
   olive oil for frying

Whisk eggs and water to a froth. Stir in mint, parsley, green onions, flour, nutmeg, and seasoning. Continue to mix well while about two inches of oil heats in a large pan. When the oil is hot enough (about 365° or when a one-inch bread cube browns in sixty seconds) drop egg mixture into the oil by spoonfuls. Brown about one minute, then turn over and continue to cook until that side has browned. Keep warm in a 200° oven until ready to serve.

KING SAMUEL'S STUFFED EGGS

 6 hard-cooked eggs
 3 tbsp. plain yogurt
 1 small onion, minced
 1 small dill pickle, minced
12 pitted black olives
    dash salt

    Slice the cooled eggs in half and remove the yolks. Mash the yolks with everything except the black olives. Fill the egg whites with the mixture and top each with an olive.

Here's another dish that's easy to put together. It actually *should* be prepared in advance, in the morning for the evening meal or the night before to be baked the next day.

SHEPHERD'S CHEESE BAKE

12 slices sourdough bread
½ cup butter
2½ cups sharp cheese, shredded
4 eggs
2 cups milk
   dash salt
½ tsp. dry mustard
   dash nutmeg

Preheat oven to 350°.

Remove crusts from bread and butter each slice. Butter a 2-quart casserole or deep baking dish. Arrange a layer of bread slices on the bottom of the dish, cutting bread where necessary to fit.

Sprinkle bread layer with a layer of grated cheese. Repeat until all bread and cheese are used, ending with a layer of cheese.

Beat eggs, milk, and seasoning together. Pour over the contents of the baking dish. Cover and store in the refrigerator overnight or for at least four hours. Sprinkle nutmeg over the top.

Bake uncovered for 40 minutes until puffed and golden brown.

ASPARAGUS RUTH

    2   cups cooked asparagus tips
    6   hard-cooked, shelled, sliced eggs
    2   tbsp. butter
 1½ tbsp. flour
    1   cup milk
        dash of salt
   ½ cup bread crumbs
    2   tbsp. butter

Preheat oven to 350°.

Prepare the sauce by melting the butter over a low heat. Blend in the flour and cook over the low heat for 3 or 4 minutes. Very slowly, stir in the milk and continue to cook and stir with a wire whisk or wooden spoon until thickened and smooth, about 10 minutes.

Place the eggs in a gratin dish, arrange asparagus tips, and pour the sauce over all. Cover with bread crumbs, dot with butter, and bake until the top has browned, about 15-20 minutes.

ONION TART HIRAM

The pie shell is made first.

    1   cup pastry flour
    ¼ tsp. salt
    ¼ lb. cold butter, cut into small pieces
    1   egg yolk
    2   tbsp. ice water

Mix flour and salt in a bowl. Cut in the butter with a pastry blender until the mixture is the size of tiny peas. Whisk egg yolk and water together in separate small bowl, add to the flour mixture, and blend until the pastry holds smoothly together. Wrap in plastic and refrigerate 20 minutes.

Preheat oven to 425°.

While the pie crust chills, prepare the filling.

Filling

    2   onions, thinly sliced
    2   cloves of garlic, minced
    3   tbsp. butter
    4   eggs
    2   cups cream or half cream and half milk
    ¼ tsp. salt
    ⅛ tsp. nutmeg
  1½ cups grated Swiss cheese

Preparation

After the pastry has chilled at least 20 minutes, pat the cold dough into a 9-inch pie pan, using the heel of your hands, pressing it over the bottom and sides of the pan. Prick the dough with a fork and then bake 10 minutes. Crust will be only partially baked.

Sauté the onions and minced garlic in butter until onions and garlic are translucent. Combine the eggs, cream, salt, and nutmeg in a bowl and whisk thoroughly. Now add the sautéed onions and grated cheese to the custard mixture, stir, and ladle into the pie crust, distributing the onions evenly.

Bake for 15 minutes at 425°; then lower the heat to 350° and bake another 40 minutes or until a knife inserted in the center comes out clean.

Chapter Six

WHOLE GRAINS AND BEANS

*So Naomi returned, and Ruth the Moabitess, her daugh-
ter in law, with her, which returned out of the country of
Moab: and they came to Bethlehem in the beginning of
barley harvest.*

(Ruth 1:22)

Barley (Hordeum vulgare), found in Stone Age dwellings, has been
cultivated for the use of man and beast since remote antiquity. It is probably the first cereal. A member of the grass family, it was grown in China at
least twenty centuries before Christ and was used as a standard for measuring weight and bartered wages. In Babylonia in 1700 B.C., Hammurabi set
down a code of laws for labor and commodities so that various work was
paid for in grain.

Barley, a small white grain with a thin brown line, is mentioned more
than thirty times in the Bible. It produces more grain per acre and needs
less irrigation than wheat.

Barley flour made from pearled barley has had the aleurone layers of
protein removed during milling. Natural brown flour, which has been
hulled but not pearled, will result in baked goods higher in protein, vitamins, and minerals. You can make your own flour by grinding the whole
grain in a food mill or coffee grinder.

A highly nutritious food, barley is mild enough to help relieve stomach
ulcers and diarrhea. It aids in preventing tooth decay and loss of hair and
strengthens fingernails.

Barley comes in two forms. Hulled barley has the outer covering removed and is best used in pilaf or as a breakfast cereal. It is more healthful

but takes about one hour or longer to cook. Pearled barley has had both the hull and the germ removed. It is cream-colored and looks like pearls. It is good steamed and buttered, has a milder flavor, and takes less time to cook.

Barley can take the place of rice, which was unknown in Bible lands.

> *Take thou also unto thee wheat, and barley, and beans, and lentiles, and millet, and fitches, and put them in one vessel, and make thee bread thereof, according to the number of the days that thou shalt lie upon thy side, three hundred and ninety days shalt thou eat thereof.*
>
> (Ezekiel 4:9)

Incidentally, "fitches" refers to the seeds of a lovely blue flower whose seeds are very spicy and were sprinkled on food like pepper.

But talking about broad beans, the fava bean (Vicia faba) is what Biblical people ate. Indeed, it fed whole populations before history began. Remains have been found in Stone Age digs.

An annual of the legume or pea family, growing to a height of three feet, the bean of history contained nearly three times more food energy and protein and a higher mineral and vitamin content than the snap bean we Americans use. Stiffly erect, it has thick, very leafy angular stems with clusters of dull white fragrant flowers, each with a blue-black spot on the wing. Up to sixteen inches long, the thick pods contain flat angular seeds larger than limas.

In ancient times the beans were used to collect votes; a white bean meant approval of the proposed measure; a black one nonsupport.

It never won the vote of Dioscorides, the Greek medical man whose *De Materia Medica* was the leading pharmacology text for sixteen centuries. He described this bean as windy, flatulent, hard of digestion, causing troublesome dreams; yet good for the cough.

If you don't have a cough and are not concerned about flatulence, other podded or dried beans may be substituted, although strictly speaking, only favas came from the old world.

In the "everything old is new again" vein, fava beans are enjoying a revival and suddenly appearing in trendy restaurants. They should. The taste is milder than limas, faintly nutty and less starchy with a light rather slippery texture that is very pleasant.

Try fresh fava beans in spring or early summer steamed whole until tender or sautéed in butter, but only when the pods are finger-thin. When the pods are medium-size, the bean pods are boiled, then the pods discarded. It's worth the trouble. Larger podded beans must be skinned as well. The beans are boiled ten to twenty minutes, then the skins are slipped off.

> *Then shall he give the rain of thy seed, that thou shalt sow the ground withal; and bread of the increase of the earth, and it shall be fat and plenteous: in that day shall thy cattle feed in large pastures. The oxen likewise and the young asses that ear the ground shall eat clean provender, which hath been winnowed with the shovel and with the fan.*
>
> (Isaiah 30:23-24)

Provender (accent on the first syllable) also known as chickpea or garbanzo (Cicer arietinum), is a bushy, hairy, annual pulse of the pea family. Relatively drought-resistant, the chickpea is not harvested before midsummer.

Seeds can be eaten boiled like peas or roasted and ground like peanuts. Sometimes they are roasted longer, and then they make a substitute for coffee. They are also grown as a field crop to feed horses. Cultivation is the same as for bush beans.

> *And it came to pass, when David was come to Mahanaim, that Shobi . . . Brought beds, and basons, and earthen vessels, and wheat, and barley, and flour, and parched corn, and beans, and lentiles, and parched pulse, and honey . . .*
>
> (II Samuel 17:27)

Lentils (Lens esculenta) are another ancient food, grown as long ago as 7000 B.C.

An annual, semi-climbing leguminous pulse, lentils thrive on poor soil and provide nourishment for poor people. Which, to paraphrase Lincoln, the Lord must have loved — He made so many of them. And fed them with soups, pastes, and purées made from lentils. Combined with other grains, it was ground into flour to make bread and cakes.

A pottage, which means any stew of vegetables or vegetables and meat, frequently was made of lentils, which is high in protein by itself, and when combined with beans is a complete protein. Bible folks may not have known that, but it didn't take them long to realize that lentils were a nourishing food that satisfied hard workers, farmers, and herdsmen. The Hebrew word for lentils is *adashim* from *adeesh* which means to tend a flock.

The little green-brown seed can be carefully split into two small curved out spheres. Its Latin name "lens" has been appropriated for that reason.

> *Judah, and the land of Israel, they were thy merchants:*
> *they traded in thy market wheat of Minnith, and pannag,*
> *and honey, and oil, and balm.*
>
> (Ezekiel 27:17)

Pannag is millet (Panicum miliaceum), related to the Latin word "*panis*" and to the French "*pain*" which of course, both mean bread. The millet plant produces more individual grains than any other. Its hard, pure white seeds make good flour. *"Miliaceum"* refers to the one thousand seeds each stem supposedly yields.

Millet, dating back to 3000 B.C. in Mesopotamia, is the best known of the family of various edible small-seeded grasses, all annual, warm season plants. Today they are most often grown as green manures and cover crops in countries that do not raise it for food, but in Mediterranean areas millet often still takes the place of oats and barley. The flour adds flavor to gravies, soups, and casseroles, but because it lacks gluten, it is mixed with wheat for making bread.

It was a staple food in China more than twelve thousand years ago and, if we're talking health, we note that it is presently eaten by the Hunza tribe living in the Himalayan foothills who are known for their health and longevity. Will eating millet work for the rest of us? It is certainly easily digested, with a good balance of amino acids and more iron than other cereals, but exuberant health and long life? Maybe that depends on whether we believe the cereal bowl is half full or half empty.

The best known of all grains, wheat, is dealt with in the chapter on bread.

BASIC BARLEY

2 cups pearled barley
4 cups water
   dash of salt
1 tbsp. butter
½ cup chopped walnuts

Rinse barley. Bring water and salt to boil. Add barley. Stir. Cover and simmer for 30 minutes. Remove from heat. Stir in butter and chopped walnuts.

CAKES OF BARLEY

3 tbsp. honey
1½ cups hot milk
3 cups barley flour
1 cup raisins
½ tsp. cinnamon
¼ tsp. salt
1 tbsp. olive oil

Heat olive oil in heavy skillet. Combine all ingredients, shape into balls, then flatten. Fry in additional hot oil five minutes on each side. Can also be baked 25 minutes in preheated 400° oven.

FAVA (OR BROAD) BEANS

Select shiny, firm bright green bean pods five to seven inches long. Pass up those with wrinkled skin or black ends. Split, the inside lining should feel moist and when you peel the bean, it tastes tender and sweet.

Only the youngest can be eaten pods and all. Inside the mature pod is a bean whose shell must be removed.

Remove beans from pods, drop into boiling water for 2 minutes, and slip off the skins. Underneath are the bright green beans. Plunge into ice water to stop the cooking. Cool, then break open the skin with your thumbnail, squeeze the bean, and the bright green fava bean will pop out.

You may be able to find cooked fava beans in cans. Or you can buy dried. To use, soak them in water for 1 hour. Drain. Cook like any other dry bean, covered with boiling water or stock, simmering approximately another 2 hours. They absorb a lot of liquid. Keep adding more boiling water as necessary. Cook until most of the water has been absorbed and the beans are tender. Then peel as directed above, season with olive oil, minced parsley, and mint.

BASIC BEANS

4 tbsp. olive oil
1 cup vegetable stock
4 tbsp. lemon juice
2 cloves minced garlic
 salt and pepper to taste
2 cups shelled fresh green fava beans
 Parmesan or other hard cheese, shaved

Warm the olive oil in a saucepan. Add the vegetable stock and bring to a boil. Add everything but the Parmesan cheese. Cook 5 minutes or until the beans are tender. Top with the shaved cheese. Drizzle more olive oil on top and serve.

MAHANAIM BEANS

5½ lbs. fava bean pods
  1   cup chicken or vegetable stock
      pinch of salt
  1   tbsp. butter
      sprig of fresh savory
  3   tbsp. butter
  2   tbsp. fresh parsley, chopped

Shell and skin the beans.

In a shallow pan, bring the stock to the boil. Add the beans, 1 tbsp. butter, salt, and savory. Boil over high heat 5 minutes uncovered.

When no more than 2 tbsp. liquid remain, the beans are done. Add the rest of the butter and chopped parsley. Stir just until the butter is melted. Adjust seasoning and serve.

FAVA BEANS CORINTHIAN

1   lb. very young fava beans (leave in pods)
    flour seasoned with salt and pepper for coating
2   tbsp. olive oil
    lemon wedges

Wash the beans, removing any strings with the tops and tails. Do not shell. Drop them into boiling, salted water. Cook rapidly for 5 minutes. Drain and pat dry.

Roll the bean pods in the seasoned flour. Pour enough olive oil in a pan to cover the bottom. Heat. Fry the beans until golden brown, turning once. Serve with lemon wedges.

OUR FAVA BEANS

4   lbs. unshelled fava beans
5   tbsp. butter
1   chopped onion
3   cloves sliced garlic
1   tsp. crushed basil
½   cup pistachio nuts
    salt and pepper to taste

   Shell the beans. Melt the butter in a saucepan, add the onion and garlic and sauté until soft. Add the beans and enough water to cover. Cook, covered, for about 15 minutes or until the beans are tender.

   Drain, saving the liquid. Put the beans in a warm oven. Return the liquid to the pan. Add the crushed basil and pistachio nuts. Turn the heat up to high. When the liquid is reduced to about ½ cup, season to taste. Pour over the beans and serve.

BAKED LENTILS LAZARUS

2   cups dried lentils
½   cup chopped onions
½   cup diced celery
½   cup carrots, chopped
3   tbsp. butter
3   tbsp. whole wheat flour
2   cups beef, chicken, or vegetable stock
¼   tsp. basil
¼   tsp. ground thyme
1   tbsp. fresh parsley, chopped
    salt to taste
¼   cup bread crumbs
½   cup Swiss cheese, shredded
    additional butter

Cook lentils in a quart of boiling water until barely tender, about 30 minutes. Drain.

While lentils are cooking, sauté vegetables in butter over low heat until tender. Stir in flour and cook one minute, stirring constantly. Whisk in stock and bring sauce to a boil. Remove from heat and add basil, thyme, and parsley. Season to taste.

Preheat oven to 375°.

When lentils are cooked, drain and stir into sauce. Spread in a shallow, buttered pan. Sprinkle with bread crumbs and cheese. Dot with butter.

Bake 40 minutes.

STEWED LENTILS

¾ lb. dried lentils, washed, picked over
1½ quarts vegetable stock
1½ whole celery stalks, chopped
 1 medium onion, chopped
 2 whole carrots, chopped
 3 cloves garlic, minced
 ½ bay leaf
    dash thyme
 ½ cup red wine

In a large soup kettle, combine all ingredients except wine and bring to a boil. Simmer over low heat for 1½ hours. Add wine and simmer 20-30 minutes more.

ESAU'S POTTAGE

2 cups brown lentils
4 cups water
1 tsp. cumin
2 large onions
¾ cup olive oil
1½ cups pearled barley
   salt and pepper to taste

Put the washed lentils in a saucepan with the water and cumin. Bring to a boil and cook 30 minutes or until almost soft.

Cut the peeled onions lengthwise in half and slice thinly. Cook half the onions in the olive oil until soft and golden. Add the washed barley, salt, pepper, and cumin to the lentils with the sautéed onions and most of the olive oil in the pan. Mix and simmer slowly another 15 minutes.

In the meantime, cook the rest of the onions very slowly in the remaining olive oil until almost caramelized.

Remove the lentil mixture from the heat, cover and let stand 10 minutes. Serve with the onions spread on top.

BASIC MILLET

½ cup hulled millet
1½-2 cups boiling water
¼ tsp. sea salt or Vege-Sal

Rinse millet. Cook, covered over low heat 20 minutes. Add salt. Let stand 20 more minutes.

Or, toast millet in large skillet until lightly browned. Add boiling water and continue as above.

APRICOT BARLEY SIDE DISH

3   tbsp. butter
1   large onion, chopped
1¼ cups pearled barley
2¾ cups vegetable stock
½   cup dried apricots, diced
½   cup almonds, chopped
¼   tsp. coriander seeds
     salt to taste

Melt the butter in a saucepan over low heat. When it starts to foam, add the onion and continue stirring. Cook about 3 minutes. Add the barley, stir into butter, then cook another 3 minutes. Pour in the stock and bring to a boil. Add the apricots, lower the heat, cover and simmer until all the water is absorbed and the barley is tender, about 20 minutes. Just before serving, stir in the almonds and coriander and season to taste.

PILAF PHILIPPIAN

  1 orange
½ lemon
  3 spring onions
1½ tbsp. butter
  1 cup barley or millet, cooked
1½ cups stock
  1 cup seedless white grapes
  1 tbsp. coriander
  1 tbsp. minced mint
     salt and pepper to taste

Remove the zest of an orange and ½ lemon. Squeeze the juice from both. Set aside.

Chop the spring onions, keeping the green and white parts separate. Melt the butter in a saucepan and cook the white scallions over low heat for a few minutes, stirring until softened. Add the cooked barley, stir, and cook another minute before adding the citrus juice and the stock. Cover and bring to a boil. Stir. Reduce heat to simmer and cook until the liquid is absorbed, about 15 minutes. Stir in the rest of the ingredients. Season to taste.

Chapter Seven

MEAT, FISH, AND POULTRY

And, thou son of man, thus saith the Lord God; Speak unto every feathered fowl, and to every beast of the field, Assemble yourselves, and come . . .

(Ezekiel 39:17)

To the ancients, meat most often meant lamb. The mature sheep, which supplied meat, milk, and wool, was the preferred animal for ancient sacrifice.

And it came to pass, that when Isaac was old, and his eyes were dim, so that he could not see, he called Esau his eldest son: and he said unto him, Behold, here am I. And he said, Behold now, I am old, I know not the day of my death: Now therefore take, I pray thee, thy weapons, thy quiver and thy bow, and go out to the field, and take me some venison; And make me savoury meat, such as I love, and bring it to me, that I may eat; that my soul may bless thee before I die.

(Genesis 27:1-4)

But, as we all know, Rebekah advised her favorite, Jacob, to deceive his father into getting his blessing:

Go now to the flock, and fetch me from thence two good kids of the goats; and I will make them savoury meat for thy father, such as he loveth: And thou shalt bring it to thy father, that he may eat, and that he may bless thee before his death.

(Genesis 27:9-10)

Cattle, goats, and sheep were domesticated by 7000 B.C. Goats were kept primarily for their milk, the surplus being made into cheese. Even horses were brought into the Tigris and Euphrates valleys as early as 2000 B.C. and were kept for food as well as for riding and pulling war chariots.

And do this thing, Take the kings away, every man out of his place, and put captains in their rooms: And number thee an army, like the army that thou hast lost, horse for horse, and chariot for chariot: and we will fight against them in the plain, and surely we shall be stronger than they.

(I Kings 20:24-25)

We have already talked about eggs from chickens, which some believe weren't really known in Bible lands until after 1000 B.C. But there are references:

O Jerusalem, Jerusalem, which killest the prophets, and stonest them that are sent unto thee; how often would I have gathered thy children together, as a hen doth gather her brood under her wings, and ye would not!

(Luke 13:34)

They also ensnared birds with small animals.

For he is cast into a net by his own feet, and he walketh upon a snare. The snare is laid for him in the ground, and a trap for him in the way.

(Job 18:8, 10)

And it came to pass, that at even the quails came up, and covered the camp: and in the morning the dew lay round about the host.

(Exodus 16:13)

If they caught wild fowl like quail, which they obviously did, how long could it have been before someone got the bright idea of penning them and their progeny?

Ducks may have been domesticated even before chickens, but geese were the first to be raised for food.

So by the time we get to Apicius, he gives us more than twenty-five recipes for cooking poultry, and many more ways to prepare fish.

> *These ye shall eat of all that are in the waters: all that have fins and scales shall ye eat:*
>
> (Deuteronomy 14:9)

Archeologists tell us that cave dwellings of prehistoric man were littered with piles of fish bones. Stone Age people used fishing implements. The Sumerians of four to six thousand years ago believed that their god provided fish for them as a special bounty.

People of the Old Testament obeyed the injunction handed down regarding the ceremonially impure shellfish without fins or scales. Every other kind of fish was kosher. They even practiced fish farming by building ponds to raise fish.

> *And they shall be broken in the purposes thereof, all that make sluices and ponds for fish.*
>
> (Isaiah 19:10)

Although we personally aren't convinced that eating flesh food is in our best interest, for those who believe the opposite, here are a few recipes using Biblical ingredients to try.

REBEKAH'S LITTLE LAMB

½ cup flour
   salt and black pepper to taste
3 lbs. lamb, cut into 2-inch cubes
½ cup olive oil
1 whole bay leaf, ¼ leaf if California bay laurel
½ tsp. each ground thyme and rosemary
2 cloves garlic
2 cups chicken stock
1¼ cups red wine
2 dozen small white onions, blanched and peeled*

Season flour with salt and pepper and dredge lamb cubes in it. Heat olive oil in large soup kettle over medium high heat. Brown lamb cubes in oil. Sprinkle herbs and garlic over lamb and add stock and wine. Simmer over medium heat for 1½ hours. Add blanched onions. Simmer ½ hour longer.

*Here's an easy way to peel these tiny onions: Drop them unpeeled into boiling water for three minutes. Rinse in cold water. Cut the root ends, then gently squeeze toward the stem end and the peeled onion pops out.

ALEXANDER'S GREAT ROAST

1   leg of lamb, about 4½ lbs.
3   cloves of garlic, peeled and sliced
    salt and freshly ground black pepper to taste
    half a lemon
1   tbsp. olive oil
2   oz. red wine mixed with 4 oz. water
2   sprigs of rosemary
¼   bay leaf

Preheat oven to 450°.

Insert slivers of garlic in slits you make in the lamb. Season with salt and pepper and rub with the lemon half. Pour the olive oil into a roasting pan before you add the meat. Brown all sides in the oven about five minutes each side.

Pour the olive oil, wine, and seasonings over the lamb. Turn the oven temperature down to 375° and continue roasting, basting occasionally, for about 2 hours.

MINT SAUCE FOR ROAST LAMB

1   tbsp. chopped fresh mint
1   tsp. honey
½   cup apple cider vinegar
4   tbsp. hot water
    salt and pepper to taste

Mix everything together and stir until the honey is dissolved.

MRS. NOAH'S CHICKEN

2   chickens, cut up into serving portions
1   cup lemon juice
2   cups bread crumbs mixed with 3 tbsp.
        grated cheese and dash of salt
1   sliced onion
    olive oil

Preheat oven to 350°.

Dip rinsed and dried chicken pieces in lemon juice, then roll in the bread crumb mixture. Place the pieces in a baking dish, then place onion slices around the chicken. Drizzle with olive oil and bake 1 hour. Serve with lemon wedges that may be squeezed over each portion just before eating.

KREPLACH

3 eggs
¾ tsp. salt
2 tbsp. water
2 cups all-purpose flour
1 small chopped onion
1 lb. cooked meat or chicken, chopped fine
1 egg
   salt and pepper to taste
¼ cup olive oil

Beat three eggs in a food processor. Add salt, water, and 1½ cups of the flour. Process (or knead by hand) until you have a medium soft dough. Divide it in half. Cover with a moist towel and set aside.

Sauté the onion and cooked meat or chicken. If there is excess fat, drain it off, then mix in one egg, salt, and pepper.

Roll out one of the dough balls until it is very thin. Cut into six 1½" squares. Place ½ teaspoon of the meat mixture in the center of each square, fold into a triangle, and press the two edges together firmly. Repeat with the second ball of dough.

Drop the kreplach into boiling water and cook, uncovered, for 15 minutes. Add to heated chicken soup.

Kreplach may also be fried and served as an appetizer.

The formed kreplach can be frozen on a cookie sheet, then transferred to plastic bags and kept in the freezer until needed.

They really had kings in those days. King Solomon was a splendid example:

 *And Solomon's provision for one day was thirty measures of fine flour, and threescore measures of meal, Ten fat oxen, and twenty oxen out of the pastures, and an hundred sheep, beside harts, and roebucks, and fallowdeer, and fatted fowl.*

(I Kings 4:22-23)

No, of course he didn't eat all that himself. With great dominion comes great responsibilities and many mouths to feed.

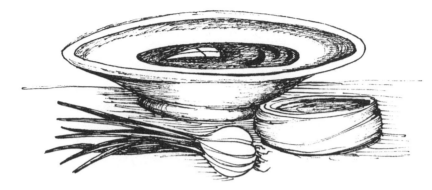

SOLOMON'S TENDERLOIN GRILL

3 cups beef stock
3 cups dry red wine
¾ cup garlic cloves, roasted
¾ cup shallots, chopped
¾ cup fresh parsley, chopped
   salt and fresh ground black pepper to taste
½ C toasted pistachios, chopped
½ cup toasted pine nuts
3 lb. beef tenderloin, cut in 8-oz steaks
3 tbsp. olive oil
6 sprigs of fresh parsley, for garnish

Preheat the grill or broiler.

Red Wine Sauce: In a large saucepan, combine the stock, red wine, 3 tablespoons of the roasted garlic, the shallots, and ¼ cup of the chopped parsley. Bring to a simmer over medium heat and cook until reduced to coat the back of a spoon, about 20 minutes. Transfer to a blender and purée until smooth. Strain through a fine sieve into another saucepan, then season with salt and pepper. Stir in the remaining parsley, then reduce heat to low.

In a small bowl, combine the remaining garlic, the toasted chopped nuts, and 2 tablespoons of the red wine sauce. Mix well.

Rub the surface of the steaks with the oil.

Grill the steaks until well-seared on the surface, about 5 minutes. Turn over and cook until you reach desired doneness, about 4 minutes for medium-rare, depending on the thickness.

Brush the tops of the steaks with a small amount of red wine sauce, then press the steaks, top side down, into the pistachio mixture, coating the surface well. Position the steaks on serving plates, spoon the remaining sauce around them, garnish with parsley sprigs, and serve.

FRICASSEE FESTUS

2½ lb. lamb cut into bite-size pieces
2 oz. unsalted butter
1 bunch spring onions, chopped
1 tbsp. chopped parsley
1 tsp. chopped mint
1 tbsp. chopped dill (or fennel)
3 heads cos lettuce (romaine), quartered
  salt and freshly ground pepper to taste

Sauce

2 egg yolks
  juice of large lemon
1 tbsp. cold water
½ pint chicken or vegetable stock

Sauté the lamb pieces in the butter. Add the onions and cook for a few more minutes. Cover with water; add seasonings and herbs. Simmer about 1½ hours or until the meat is tender. Add the lettuce and cook 15 minutes. Drain off the liquid and save. Transfer the meat to a serving dish and keep warm.

The Sauce: Using a whisk, beat the egg yolks with the lemon juice in a bowl until frothy. Add the tablespoon of cold water and beat.

Boil the stock. Allow to cool for three minutes. Pour a spoonful of the stock into the egg and lemon mixture, whisking while adding two more spoonfuls. Very gradually, add the rest of the stock, beating all the time until it thickens. Pour the sauce over the lamb and lettuce.

POMEGRANATE KIDNEYS

12 lamb kidneys, trimmed, skinned and cut in half lengthwise
½ lb. unsalted butter
2 cloves crushed garlic
    salt and freshly ground pepper to taste
½ tsp. cinnamon
½ cup pomegranate juice (can be bought at Middle Eastern shops)
1 tbsp. finely chopped parsley

Sauté the kidneys with the garlic in the melted butter. Add salt and spices, stirring. Add pomegranate juice. Simmer about 5 minutes with minced parsley.

NOAH'S PHEASANT

3 2-lb. pheasants
½ cup olive oil
½ cup lemon juice
6 cloves garlic, peeled and chopped
8 oz. butter
½ cup flour
4 oz. pine nuts
8 oz. green grapes, cut in halves
4 shallots
1 cup heavy cream
1 cup dry sherry

With a sharp knife, remove the breasts from the center bone and also all the meat from the legs. Remove all the skin and excess fat. Place the pheasant breasts and leg meat in a ceramic dish. Reserve the bones for another dish.

Marinate breasts with the garlic, lemon juice, and olive oil, overnight.

Melt the butter in a heavy skillet, season the pheasant with salt and pepper, dip in flour, and sauté over low heat until light brown. Remove from skillet and place pheasant on a heated platter.

Add more butter to the pan, if necessary, and add the shallots and simmer. Combine with sherry wine, heavy cream, and grapes and bring to a boil. Garnish with pine nuts and ladle over the pheasants.

PRIESTLY CHICKEN WITH LEEKS

3 2-lb. chickens, boned
½ cup butter
1 small carrot, chopped
1 small onion, chopped
3 tbsp. shallots, minced
3 cups dry white wine
¼ cup cognac
1 tsp. fresh thyme
3 cups chicken stock
¼ cup heavy whipping cream
   salt and pepper to taste
   additional 4 tbsp. butter
1 lb. leeks, cleaned and julienned
½ lb. seedless green grapes, halved

Bone the chicken; set aside the meat. Chop the bones and sauté in ½ cup butter until browned. Add the carrot, onion, and shallots; sauté a few minutes. Add wine, cognac and chopped thyme.

Reduce liquid to ½ cup. Add chicken stock; reduce to 1½ cup. Remove the bones. Add cream, bring to a boil, and strain. Season to taste. Keep warm.

Preheat oven to 400°. Sauté the chicken in 3 tablespoons butter. Transfer to oven with pan drippings and bake for 15 minutes. Remove the chicken and tent with foil.

Using the pan juice, sauté leeks for 5 minutes and remove. Using remaining 1 tablespoon butter, sauté grapes for 1 minute to heat.

To assemble, divide leeks among 6 plates. Place chicken atop leeks. Add sauce and garnish with grapes.

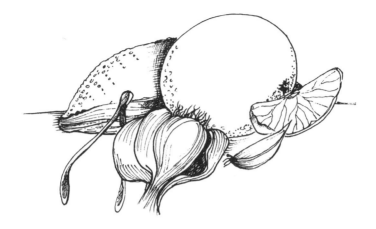

CHICKEN EZRA

6 large chicken breasts, boned and skinned
1½ tbsp. flour
2¼ tbsp. olive oil
4½ cloves garlic, halved
½ bay leaf, crushed
3 tbsp. honey
½ cup dry white wine
    juice of 1 lemon
    juice of 1 orange
    salt to taste
    24 x 17-inch sheet of foil
3 tbsp. pine nuts

Flour chicken breasts; set aside. In a 12-inch nonstick pan, heat olive oil over a medium-high heat and sauté breasts with garlic and crushed bay leaf until chicken is golden (about 12½ minutes per side). Remove breasts from pan and set aside.

Add honey and wine to pan; reduce mixture by half. Add juices, salt, and reduce again by two-thirds. Discard garlic.

Preheat oven to 450°.

Place buttered foil on a shallow roasting pan. Place chicken on one-half of the foil. Add pine nuts and spoon sauce over breasts. Fold foil over the top of the chicken. Crimp the edges together until you have an airtight seal. Place in the oven for 12 minutes. Remove promptly and serve.

CHICKEN PILAF

1   (4-5 lb.) chicken, cut in pieces, skin removed
1   medium onion, sliced
1   sliced carrot
1   stalk celery
3   cloves garlic
½   bay leaf
½   tsp. thyme
½   tsp. cumin
    salt to taste
1   cinnamon stick

Put chicken in pot with vegetables and water to cover. Add bay leaf, thyme, and cumin. Bring to boil. Skim foam. Season to taste with salt. Add cinnamon stick. Reduce heat and simmer until meat easily comes off bones, about 1 hour.

Take pot from stove and use slotted spoon to remove meat to a bowl. Reserve cooking liquid. When cool enough to handle, remove meat from bones. Discard bones. Set meat aside.

The chicken and broth may be cooked a day ahead. The meat is then easier to remove from the bone and the fat easier to skim from the stock.

Pilaf

2 cups barley
5 tbsp. butter
  reserved chicken cooking liquid, strained
½ cup blanched or sliced almonds
¼ cup pine nuts
  salt to taste
2 tbsp. flour
  yogurt, optional

Soak barley in pot of hot water to cover for ½ hour. Drain and rinse with cold water. Melt 2 tablespoons butter in pan, add barley, and sauté gently, stirring constantly, until water is gone and grains are coated with butter.

Skim off any fat from chicken cooking liquid. Measure out 4 cups cooking liquid and pour into pot with barley. (Reserve remaining cooking liquid to make gravy.) Bring to boil. Cook until barley is tender and stock is absorbed, about 20 minutes. Taste and add salt.

Melt 1 tablespoon butter in pan. Add almonds and pine nuts. Sauté over medium heat until golden. Add a dash of salt. Immediately pour nuts into bowl to prevent further cooking.

Measure reserved cooking liquid for gravy. If there is more than ½ cup, boil down. If there is less, add water to make ½ cup. Melt remaining 2 tablespoons butter in pan. Stir in 2 tablespoons flour. Cook until brown. Stir in stock and cook until thickened. Add chicken meat and toss to mix.

Arrange nuts in bottom of well-oiled deep round bowl. Fill bowl with cooked barley and press down gently. Then arrange the chicken pieces, add more barley and nuts. Press everything down. Now place a serving platter, upside-down, over the bowl. Hold it down as you turn bowl and platter together rightside-up. When you remove the bowl, you'll have a molded pilaf on the serving platter.

Alternatively, divide nuts and barley into soup bowls and unmold individually on plates. Top barley with chicken pieces and serve. Pass yogurt as garnish.

If you prefer not to serve right away, refrigerate. Half an hour before serving, brush a little olive oil over the exposed portion and warm in a 350° oven for 20-25 minutes. Remove from heat and carefully unmold as instructed above.

HAGAR'S HONEY CHICK

    2   small fryers, cut up
    2   cups buttermilk
    1   cup honey
 1½ cups bread crumbs
    1   tbsp. chopped parsley
  ½   tsp. basil
  ½   tsp. thyme
    1   tsp. sea salt
 3-4 tbsp. olive oil

Soak chicken pieces in buttermilk one hour. Drain and pat dry.

With a pastry brush, brush each piece of chicken with honey. Mix bread crumbs with spices, sprinkle over chicken. Heat olive oil in heavy skillet. Add chicken pieces in a single layer. Cook over medium heat, turning as they brown. Cover skillet and turn down heat, simmering until chicken is done, ten to fifteen minutes.

Send the multitude away, that they may go into the villages, and buy themselves victuals. But Jesus said unto them, They need not depart; give ye them to eat. And they say unto him, We have here but five loaves, and two fishes. He said, Bring them hither to me. And he commanded the multitude to sit down on the grass, and took the five loaves, and the two fishes, and looking up to heaven, he blessed, and brake, and gave the loaves to his disciples, and the disciples to the multitude. And they did all eat, and were filled: and they took up of the fragments that remained twelve baskets full. And they that had eaten were about five thousand men, beside women and children.

(Matthew 14:15-21)

FILLETS OF SOLE EN VINO E GRAPPE

1 tsp. salt
2 lbs. St. Peter's fish (John Dory) fillets
1 cup seedless green grapes
¾ cup dry white wine
1 cup heavy cream
1 cup fresh figs

Preheat oven to 450°.

Butter a shallow baking dish. Place fish in a single layer, slightly overlapping. Salt the fish. Add grapes and pour wine over the grapes and fillets. Bake 12-15 minutes. Heat the cream in a saucepan. When the fish is done, spoon 6 tablespoons of the baking liquid into the hot cream and whisk until blended. Transfer the fillets to a warm platter. Add the grapes and figs and pour on the cream sauce. Serve with a few more grapes on each portion.

SIMON'S FISH KEBAB

2½ lbs. firm white fish, such as swordfish or halibut, filleted

Marinade

4 cloves crushed garlic
2 pounded anchovy fillets
½ cup water
½ cup white wine
3 tbsp. white wine vinegar
  juice of 1 lemon
½ crushed bay leaf
½ tbsp. finely chopped parsley
  dash thyme

Cut fish into bite-sized cubes. Mix all marinade ingredients. Marinate fish at least 2 hours.

Note: Soak skewers in water for one-half hour before assembling.

Skewer fish and grill, turning and basting frequently with the marinade until brown on the outside. Serve with quartered lemons and homemade bread.

FISH OF GALILEE

2½ lbs. fish steaks or fillets

or

6 cleaned, small whole fish such as trout or salmon*

2 slices toasted bread

2 tbsp. Parmesan cheese

⅓ tsp. dry thyme

dash of salt

4 tbsp. melted butter

*A medium dense, flaky-fleshed fish works for this recipe.

Preheat oven to 425°. Rinse fish, pat dry.

Cheese-crumb coating: Whirl the toasted bread (sourdough or whole wheat) in a blender or food processor until crumbed. Mix crumbs with Parmesan cheese, thyme, and a dash of salt.

Pour melted butter into a shallow dish. Coat fish in butter, then dip in cheese-crumb coating. Place fish in a foil-lined shallow baking pan. Bake 10 to 15 minutes or until fish is just opaque, but still moist in the thickest part.

The fowl of the air, and the fish of the sea, (and whatsoever) passeth through the paths of the seas . . .

(Psalms 8:8)

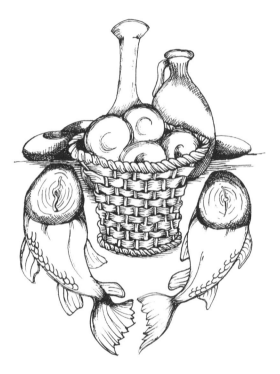

PETER'S FISH

2 lbs. fish fillets
2 tbsp. butter
3 shallots finely chopped
1 clove minced garlic
¼ cup chicken broth
¼ cup dry white wine
½ cup artichoke hearts (marinated)

Rinse fish, pat dry.

Melt butter in large frying pan over medium heat. Add shallots and garlic. Stir and cook until soft. Add broth and wine and bring to a boil. Arrange fish in a single layer, add artichoke hearts, reduce heat, cover, and simmer until fish is barely done, 5-7 minutes. Remove fish and artichokes. Arrange on a platter. Bring pan juices to a boil, then boil until slightly thickened. Spoon sauce over fish.

ALMOND FISHES

6 trout, cleaned and boned
    salt to taste
    cracked pepper
½ cup butter
½ cup ground almonds
    juice of 1 small lemon

Season the trout with salt and pepper. Melt the butter in a frying pan and fry the trout on each side for about 6 minutes or until golden brown and cooked through. Remove from the pan, place on a heated serving dish, and keep warm. Sauté the almonds in the butter left in the pan until they are golden. Add the lemon juice, mix well, and spoon over the fish.

SALMON LATKES

1½ lbs. boneless, skinless salmon fillet
 1   medium onion
 1   stalk celery
 3   sprigs parsley
 2   tbsp. chopped fresh dill
½ tsp. salt
    dash cayenne pepper
 1   tbsp. fresh lemon juice
 3   eggs
 1   additional egg white
1½ cups dry bread crumbs
½ cup oil

Place salmon in food processor with onion, celery, parsley, dill, salt, and cayenne. Process briefly so the mixture is chopped, not puréed. Add the lemon juice, eggs and extra egg white and one-third of the bread crumbs. Combine.

Form into three-inch patties and dip into remaining bread crumbs, coating both sides.

Heat about one-third cup of oil in a large frying pan. Fry latkes until golden brown, using additional oil for each batch. Drain on paper towels, keeping warm in a 250° oven until ready to serve.

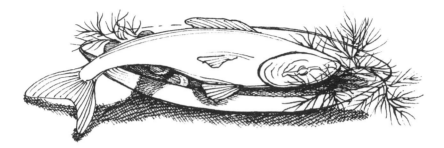

HONEY WALNUT TROUT

```
 4  tbsp. butter
 3  onions, thinly sliced
 2  cloves garlic
 2  tsp. ground cumin
    salt and freshly ground pepper to taste
1½  cups finely chopped walnuts
 2  tbsp. honey
 2  tbsp. water
⅔  cup dry white wine
 6  fresh trout, filleted
```

Preheat oven to 325°

Generously butter a baking dish. Melt half the butter in a saucepan over medium heat and soften the sliced onions and garlic in it for 6–7 minutes.

Stir in the cumin, salt, pepper, and walnuts. Add the honey, 2 tbsp. water, and the wine, and gently simmer for 3–4 minutes.

Arrange the onions and walnuts in a layer on the bottom of the baking dish. Season the trout lightly and arrange on top. Dot with the rest of the butter. Cover and bake for 25 minutes or until the fish flakes when tested.

Transfer the fish to a warmed serving dish. Pour the juices over the trout and serve.

Chapter Eight

BREAD

So Hiram gave Solomon cedar trees and fir trees according to all his desire. And Solomon gave Hiram twenty thousand measures of wheat for food to his household, and twenty measures of pure oil: thus gave Solomon to Hiram year by year.

(I Kings 5:10-11)

Bread is mentioned more times in the Bible than any other food. The main field crop in Biblical times was wheat, the queen of grains, the most universally grown of all, sown in almost every part of the earth. The domestication of wheat, one of the earliest plants cultivated, took place about eight thousand years ago in the Assyrian mountains and perhaps in the Holy Land as well.

In Pharaoh's dream of seven ears of corn on one stalk, it is generally agreed that his dream referred to a composite wheat with seven heads on each stalk. Biblical translators often used the word corn instead of wheat or grain. Indian maize was unknown in Bible days. Joseph, who interpreted the dream with its seven lean years of famine, was the first to advise storing surplus wheat in granaries. Before that, wheat was kept in storerooms in the center of the house where it could stay dry. Early in man's history, he found that wheat could be boiled to kill insects and their eggs, then sun-dried to preserve it. This processed wheat is known as bulgur, which today is steamed, then dried and coarsely milled. It comes with a hearty flavor and high nutrition. Because it is dried, it must be soaked in liquid for an hour if used raw (in salads) but not when cooked. Use one part of bulgur to two parts water in soups, stuffings, salads, and breakfast cereals.

And Boaz said unto her, At mealtime come thou hither, and eat of the bread, and dip thy morsel in the vinegar. And she sat beside the reapers: and he reached her parched corn, and she did eat, and was sufficed, and left.

(Ruth 2:14)

Wheat is a member of the Grass family. All species are annuals with erect stems ending in an ear of spikelets, each of which has three to seven flowers. Only a few produce grains. These consist of a single seed or embryo, called the germ, the most vital part of the plant, the only one capable of producing a new plant, and includes the greatest amount of vitamins and minerals. The endosperm surrounds the germ and contains gluten-forming proteins and starch. Around the endosperm is a layer of aleurone, another protein, then several layers of bran. A thin husk surrounds the entire seed.

To turn grain into flour, the Egyptian millers removed the husk and pulverized the germ and endosperm between huge stones. Since only the husk was removed, the flour contained all the nutrients in the grain including the wheat germ and the wheat germ oil.

Bread was obviously the basic cereal food. At various times, depending on the social strata and whether the harvest was bountiful or plagued, the wheat flour was increased in bulk by adding other grains, ground beans or various plant material.

Egyptians experimented with yeast-fermented doughs and are known to have had at least fifteen kinds of bread, some sweetened with honey. They had professional millers and bakers by 2000 B.C., and we have pictures showing them kneading dough with their feet. Their loaves were triangular or in long rolls. In Rome barley bread was for the common folks while the upper classes feasted on wheat bread. Their cakes and pastry came in all shapes and sizes, probably to match their feet.

Egyptian bakers often used reserved sourdough to make leavened loaves. The wild yeast in the bread also helped in the beer-making process. Beer was the country's national drink, often carried to the fields in clay jugs as a thirst quencher. Brewers soaked half-baked bread in water and then added date juice to sweeten the liquid and hasten fermentation.

Incidentally, beer, which the Greeks and Romans considered a barbarian drink, was not brewed with hops until medieval times when herbs were added to beer to provide flavor and preserve it. Of all the herbs used, the hop became the one most preferred.

When buying whole wheat flour, whether pastry or bread flour, look for stone-ground 100 percent whole wheat, preferably organically grown without chemical fertilizers or pesticide sprays.

METHUSELAH'S EGG BREAD

1 pkg. dry yeast
¼ cup warm water (105°)
2 eggs
2 cups scalded milk (cool to 105°)
2 tbsp. melted butter
2 tsp. salt
2 tbsp. date sugar (or 1 tbsp. honey)
6-6½ cups regular all-purpose flour (sift before measuring)
3 tbsp. olive oil

Pour yeast into a bowl, add water and stir until dissolved.

Break 2 eggs into a 2-cup measure. Beat in scalded and cooled milk to make 2 cups.

Add the melted butter, salt and sugar or honey. Stir until well blended. Add 3 cups of flour, a little at a time. Add a 4th cup and beat until dough is smooth and elastic. Mix in the 5th cup of flour to make a stiff dough.

Measure the 6th cup of flour and sprinkle about half of it on the board. Turn out dough onto heavily floured area of the board. Keep a coating of flour on the dough as you begin to knead with floured hands. Add more flour to board until the dough no longer sticks.

When dough is smooth and satiny, put it in a bowl oiled with part of the olive oil. Use the rest to lightly oil the top of the dough. Cover with a clean towel and let rise in a warm place (about 80°) for about 1-1½ hours. Dough should have risen to almost double in size. Test by inserting two fingers ½ inch into the risen dough. If the indentations remain, the dough is ready to shape.

Punch dough down and squeeze out all the air bubbles. Divide the dough in half, then divide each half into 3 parts. Roll each into a strand and braid three strands together, pinching ends to seal.

Let the two loaves rise on a lightly oiled (or buttered) baking sheet. Let rise in a warm place another 45 minutes or until dough has again almost doubled.

Preheat oven to 350°.

Brush tops with slightly beaten egg and bake 30-35 minutes or until nicely browned.

Yet a little sleep, a little slumber, a little folding of the hands to sleep:

(Proverbs 6:10)

BASIC BULGUR OR CRACKED WHEAT

Use 1 cup of bulgur to 2 cups of water and ¼ teaspoon salt. Combine in saucepan and bring to a boil. Let simmer until the water is absorbed (about 15 minutes). For cracked wheat, cook longer, about 25-30 minutes or until the water is absorbed.

A LITTLE LOAF

1 pkg. dry yeast
¼ cup warm milk (105°)
1 tbsp. honey
2 cups unbleached all-purpose flour
1 tsp. salt
½ cup frozen butter, cut into small pieces
2 eggs, lightly beaten
   olive oil
1 beaten egg
1 tbsp. milk

Pour yeast into a bowl, add milk and honey. Stir until dissolved.

Using your food processor, add flour, salt, and butter, then pulse until the butter is cut into the flour. Add the yeast mixture and combine briefly. Add eggs until a ball of dough forms. Turn out onto a lightly floured breadboard and knead, incorporating more flour until the mixture holds together and is smooth.

Turn into a bowl that has been oiled with the olive oil. Turn the dough to coat all sides. Cover and let rise in a warm place 1½ to 2 hours.

Preheat oven to 350°.

Punch down, knead several times, then shape into a loaf. Place in a well-buttered loaf pan. Cover again and let rise until doubled, about 1 hour. Brush with a glaze made by beating 1 egg with 1 tablespoon of milk or cream. Bake 35-40 minutes.

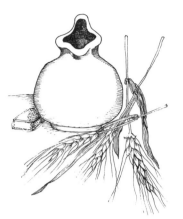

SWEET ANISE CHALLAH

 1 pkg. yeast
¼ cup warm water
⅓ cup each butter, honey, and milk
½ tsp. salt
3½ cups unbleached flour, sifted
 1 egg, slightly beaten
 2 tbsp. orange juice
 1 tsp. orange peel, shredded
 3 tsp. anise seed

Soften the yeast in the warm water. In a separate saucepan, scald milk by bringing it just to a boil. Add butter, honey, and salt to the saucepan, stirring until the butter melts. Cool to lukewarm. Add 1 cup of the sifted flour, beat well. Add yeast, egg, orange juice, orange peel, and anise seed. Beat well. Add the rest of the flour.

Turn out on lightly floured surface, knead until smooth and elastic (8-10 minutes). Place in lightly greased bowl, turning once to oil the surface. Cover and let double in a warm place, about 1½ hours.

Punch down. Let rest 10 minutes.

Divide into four pieces. Roll into strands. Braid three strands together, pinching ends to seal and pulling the braids tight; then bring two ends together, forming a circle. Divide the fourth section into three strands, braid and place on top of round loaf. Place on oiled cookie sheet. Cover. Let double about 45 minutes.

Preheat oven to 350°.

Brush tops with egg wash (one egg mixed with 2 tbsp. water).

Bake 35-40 minutes. Place tented foil over the top for the last 20 minutes. Test for doneness by inserting a straw or cake tester. When it emerges, clean, remove loaf from pan, and cool.

EASY ROLLS

1 pkg. yeast
1 cup warm water
2 tbsp. honey
1 tsp. salt
1 egg, beaten
3 cups unbleached whole wheat flour
4 tbsp. olive oil

Dissolve yeast in the water. Add honey, salt, and beaten egg. Stir well, then let stand while you sift the flour twice. Add oil and half the flour to the yeast mixture. Beat until very smooth. Add remaining flour and blend well. Set dough in a warm place and allow to rise until almost doubled in bulk, about 30 minutes.

Drop dough by the spoonful into small greased muffin pans so each cup is half full. Let rise until almost doubled in bulk.

Preheat oven to 400°.

Bake for 15 minutes. Makes two dozen rolls.

Variations

After the dough has risen, divide into four parts and place each part in a bowl with one of the following:

4 tbsp. chopped raisins
4 tbsp. chopped walnuts
4 tbsp. chopped almonds
¼ cup shredded Swiss or Parmesan cheese
1 tbsp. carob powder mixed with 1 tbsp. honey

Mix each portion of dough with the added ingredient until well blended. Then proceed with the basic recipe.

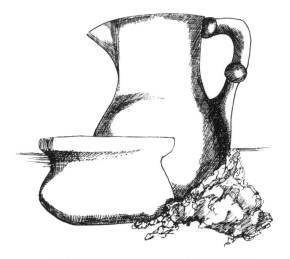

GIDEON'S CHEESE ROLLS

  1   pkg. yeast, not instant
 ¼ cup warm water
  4   cups all-purpose flour
 ½ tsp. salt
 ⅔ cup yogurt
 ½ cup honey
 ½ cup olive oil
  6   egg yolks
 ¼ cup milk
2¼ cups shredded sharp Cheddar cheese
 ⅓ cup melted butter

Dissolve the yeast in the warm water. Sift flour and salt together. Into the yeast mixture stir yogurt, honey, and ½ cup flour mixture. Cover and let rise in warm place for about 20 minutes, until doubled in size.

Add olive oil, mix well. Add egg yolks one at a time, beating very well after each one. Beat in the remaining flour and milk. Stir in the yeast mixture and beat until smooth.

Turn the dough out onto a lightly floured surface and divide into 12 parts. Roll each part into an 8-inch circle. Sprinkle 2 tablespoons of the cheese onto each circle. Roll circles like a jelly roll and coil into crescent shape. Place on ungreased baking sheets. Cover and let rise in warm place until doubled in size, about 1 to 1½ hours.

Preheat the oven to 400° and bake the rolls for 15 to 20 minutes or until golden brown.

Remove from oven and immediately brush with some melted butter and sprinkle on remaining cheese. Serve while warm. Yields 12 large crescents.

ROSEMARY LOAVES

    1 tsp. honey
    1 cup warm water
    1 pkg. dry yeast
    1½ cups unbleached white bread flour
    1½ cups whole wheat bread flour
    1½ tsp. kosher salt
    1 tbsp. fresh rosemary, finely chopped
    3 tbsp. extra-virgin olive oil
       additional olive oil and kosher salt

Mix the honey in the warm water. Stir in the yeast. Leave in a warm place until foamy, about 10 minutes.

Meanwhile, measure the flour and salt into a large mixing bowl. Add the chopped rosemary.

Add the olive oil to the yeast mixture, stir, then pour into the flour and salt. Mix until the dough forms.

Turn the dough out onto a flat, lightly floured surface and knead until the dough is smooth and elastic, adding more flour when necessary.

Place the dough in a clean, lightly oiled bowl and turn once to coat with oil. Cover with plastic wrap and let rise in a warm place about 30-40 minutes until double in volume.

Turn the dough out onto a lightly floured board and roll with a rolling pin into 1 large or 2 small ovals ½ inch thick. Using a sharp knife, make several crisscrossed diagonal cuts on the tops of the ovals and then pull the cut edges slightly apart.

Lightly oil a baking sheet. Place the loaves on the baking sheet, brushing the tops with olive oil. Sprinkle with salt. Cover and let rise again in a warm place about 20 minutes or doubled in volume.

Preheat oven to 450°.

Bake the loaves 25-30 minutes. They are ready when golden brown and make a hollow sound when tapped. Cool loaves on a wire rack.

Like the discovery of fire, blundering into the uses of sourdough cookery was most likely accidental. In the days of the pharaohs, an Egyptian baker may have noticed that some batter he had left out and forgotten had mysteriously formed bubbles. When added to a new batch of bread, the loaves had a zesty aroma and a tangy flavor the earlier efforts lacked.

Skipping a few thousand years and not being as smart as that Egyptian baker, I was totally intimidated by the idea of making sourdough bread, especially when my first loaves were more than sour. Now I believe I know what went wrong; I didn't start with unbleached all-purpose flour for the starter. Once you pass the starter phase and have developed the gluten, adding whole wheat or rye works just fine.

Sourdough cookery is simple, but a lot depends on the starter. It's like a bank. Once you make the initial deposit, you withdraw some for your current use, replace what you spent by returning an equal sum (of flour and water), let it sit overnight in the "vault" (the warm place, covered with plastic wrap and maybe also a towel), then store it once more in the refrigerator. If you don't use it again within a week, add ½ cup of flour and ½ cup of warm water to the starter, leave it out overnight in the warm area, stir down, and return to the refrigerator.

Occasionally, you must pour the starter into another container while you wash the original one to remove the flour, which has crusted around the bowl. If the starter isn't as bubbly as it was before, sprinkle in about half a package of yeast and mix. The only thing to be aware of is if it ever develops a strange orange or pink color or has an unfriendly smell—in which case, discard the whole thing and start over. It sounds complicated, but it isn't, and the tangy, zesty taste of a sourdough loaf is worth extra effort.

BASIC SOURDOUGH STARTER

1   pkg. dry yeast
2   cups lukewarm water
1   tbsp honey
2   cups all-purpose unbleached flour
1   tsp. salt

Dissolve yeast in water in glass or pottery bowl. Add honey. Set aside for ten minutes until it is frothy. With a wooden spoon, stir in the flour and salt until the mixture resembles a smooth paste.

Cover with a towel or plastic wrap and place in warm (80-85°) draft-free area. A pilot-lighted gas oven is perfect or the enclosed space next to a water heater. Stir with a wooden spoon several times a day. In 36-48 hours your starter will be slightly bubbly with a pleasantly clean, yeasty aroma.

Either use in a recipe right away or transfer to a plastic container, cover with a lid that you've punched a hole in so the gases can escape. Refrigerate until needed.

DANIEL'S SOURDOUGH LOAF

½ cup butter
⅓ cup honey
1 cup sourdough starter
1 cup lukewarm milk
3 eggs, beaten
1 tsp. sea salt
4-4½ cups unbleached all-purpose flour

In a large mixing bowl or food processor, cream together butter and honey. Add sourdough starter and pulse or mix together. With processor or mixer going, slowly alternate adding milk and beaten eggs. Add salt and flour. Beat until smooth. If using a food processor, transfer batter to a large bowl. Place, covered, in a warm, draft-free place and let it rise until doubled in size.

Stir down, then pour into two greased bread pans. Let rise again until once more doubled in size.

Preheat oven to 325°.

Bake 45 minutes or until golden brown. Makes two loaves.

POCKETS OF THE SPHINX

Using Daniel's basic recipe, turn dough out on a floured surface. With floured hands, knead dough, adding more flour and incorporating it into the dough.

When it holds together and has a satiny appearance, divide dough into 16 small pieces. Roll between your floured hands, shaping each piece into a ball. Cover with a towel and let sit in a warm place until doubled in bulk.

Preheat oven to 375°.

Roll out each ball of dough with a rolling pin on a floured surface making a circle ¼ inch thick and evenly flat. Place on unoiled baking sheet and bake 10 minutes.

NOT FOR PROPHET BREAD

1	pkg. dry yeast
3	tbsp. warm water
3	tbsp. honey
2	cups sourdough starter
1	tsp. salt
2	tbsp. olive oil
3	tbsp. cream
3½-4	cups unbleached flour
1	cup shredded Cheddar cheese
½	cup sliced onion
2	tbsp. melted butter
	additional oil and butter

Dissolve yeast in warm water with honey in large bowl. Add starter with salt, oil, and cream. Gradually add flour, stirring with wooden spoon, until mixture pulls away from sides of bowl. Turn out onto a floured surface and knead 5-7 minutes until smooth. Sauté onion in butter.

Roll out dough to an 8" x 10" rectangle. Sprinkle with cheese and sautéed onions. Roll up like a jelly roll, starting with the narrow side. Place in oiled loaf pan. Brush top with oil. Cover with a cloth, place in warm, draft-free place. Let rise until doubled in size.

Preheat oven to 350°.

Bake for 50 minutes or until done. Brush top with melted butter. Makes one loaf.

RAISIN CAIN

1   cup sourdough starter
¼   cup lukewarm milk
¼   cup honey
¼   cup melted butter
1   tsp. salt
1   beaten egg
1½ tsp. cinnamon
½   tsp. anise extract (optional)
½   cup chopped walnuts
1   cup raisins
2   cups unbleached flour

With the sourdough starter in a large mixing bowl, add milk, honey, butter, salt, egg, cinnamon, anise, and mix thoroughly. Add nuts. Combine raisins and flour. Gradually add to batter while stirring. Cover with a cloth. Place in warm, draft-free place. Let rise about 1 hour or until doubled in size. Stir batter down. Place in oiled nine-inch loaf pan. Let rise again.

Preheat oven to 350°. Bake for 40-45 minutes or until golden brown. Makes 1 loaf.

WHOLLY PANCAKES

This must be started the night before:

    1 tbsp. dry yeast
    2 cups lukewarm water
  1½ cups whole wheat flour
   ½ cup unbleached pastry flour
    1 cup sourdough starter

Day two:

    2 beaten eggs
   ¾ tsp. sea salt
    1 tbsp. honey

Night before: Soften the yeast in ½ cup of the water. Allow it to bubble, then add the rest of the water. Add both kinds of flour. Beat well and pour into a large pitcher with enough space on top for it to rise. Cover and store in warm place overnight.

The next morning stir down the batter. Remove 1 cupful and return to sourdough starter. Add the rest of the ingredients. Mix well and pour onto a hot griddle. Serves 4-6.

Here's a variation on an old favorite. There's absolutely no reason why Bible people *couldn't* have prepared them, but they probably didn't. We can, using their ingredients. The addition of cheese makes the crust tasty and chewy.

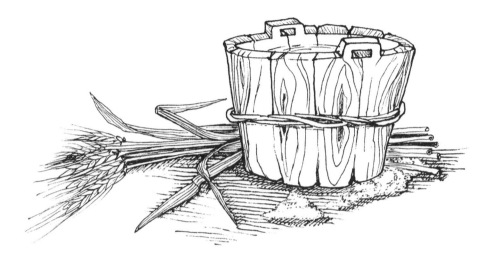

CHEESED POPOVERS

1 cup unbleached pastry flour, sifted
¼ tsp. salt
1 tbsp. melted butter
2 eggs, beaten
1 cup milk
½ cup grated Cheddar cheese
    additional butter or olive oil to grease muffin tins

In a bowl, mix flour with salt. Add butter, eggs, and milk. Beat until very smooth, scraping bowl frequently. Add cheese. Mix until just blended.

Pour into well-buttered muffin tins, filling ⅔ full. Place in a cold oven, setting the heat to 450°. Bake 15 minutes, reduce heat to 350° and bake another 15-20 minutes.

Chapter Nine

FRUITS AND NUTS

And it came to pass that on the morrow Moses went into the tabernacle of witness; and, behold, the rod of Aaron for the house of Levi was budded, and brought forth buds, and bloomed blossoms, and yielded almonds.

(Numbers 17:8)

A flowering almond tree is one of God's miracles. First to bloom even before the end of winter, earlier than the peach tree, which it resembles and to which it is related, the almond tree (Prunus amygdalus) heralds spring everywhere just as it did in Bible lands. Pink or white lightly perfumed flowers appear on bare branches for about a month and symbolize the continuation of life after winter's barren span.

A close relative of the plum and peach, the almond fruit starts to ripen about ten weeks after the flowers appear. The shell of the nut is encased in a wrinkled, leathery coat, which is really the pit of the small peach-like but inedible fruit.

The high fat, carbohydrate, and protein content explains why almonds have been a valuable food for centuries.

Their excellent vitamin B_2 and calcium elements benefit teeth and bones. Dioscorides recommended ground almonds in a poultice to take away spots in the face that were caused by sunburning. Almond oil is still a popular ingredient in fine face creams.

The vine is dried up, and the fig tree languisheth; the pomegranate tree, the palm tree also, and the apple tree, even all the trees of the field, are withered: because joy is withered away from the sons of men.

(Joel 1:12)

Apples are mentioned several times in the Bible.

> *As the apple tree among the trees of the wood, so is my beloved among the sons. I sat down under his shadow with great delight, and his fruit was sweet to my taste.*
>
> (Song of Solomon 2:3)

and

> *Stay me with flagons, comfort me with apples: for I am sick of love.*
>
> (Song of Solomon 2:5)

Despite these references, some Biblical botanists seriously doubt they were apples, claiming the ancient language referred to apricot or bitter orange (citron) instead, although those plants were introduced much later than the apple (Malus sylvestris), which dates from the Neolithic Age. Some claim that the forbidden fruit that Adam and Eve tasted was not the apple but the grape — and the fermented variety at that.

But the Sumerians who lived in the Holy Land long before 2000 B.C. mention them. Apples may have been native to Lebanon, too, or introduced into Israel and Egypt from Iran or Armenia about 4000 B.C. Ancient Egyptian papyri from 1298-1235 B.C. state that the fields of the Nile delta were full of pomegranate, apple, olive, and fig trees.

The Hittites cultivated apple trees. Their law demanded a payment of six shekels of silver from any man who destroyed an apple tree, a considerable sum in those days. The Greek Theophrastus, born in 370 B.C., described many kinds of apples. It may be that the Bible's apple was similar to a crab apple, but it appears that the apple in whatever form was appreciated by the ancients. They may even have known that the pectin in apple peels lowers blood cholesterol and the large number of minerals and vitamins is generally strengthening.

The stately apple tree, covered with snowy blossoms in spring, has developed the largest number of varieties of any fruit raised. At the moment, it is somewhere in the neighborhood of over seven thousand and, for all we know, still increasing. The fruit, the juice — it's hard to imagine life without it.

> *A word fitly spoken is like apples of gold in pictures of silver.*
>
> (Proverbs 25:11)

But the "golden apples" describes apricots in this case, not apples. Indeed, the Greeks called them golden apples and stayed out of the argument when some authorities maintained that the apples in the Bible referred to apricots. According to the scholars, Eve may have been banished from the Garden of Eden after biting into a forbidden apricot. Or an orange. Professors also pointed to the pomegranate as the First Fruit. Others just as stoutly declared that the evidence indicated it *was* an apple.

The only thing that's certain is that ripe apricots are divine and did exist in Bible lands. They may have been initially grown in the orchards of Mesopotamia, the ancient land between the Tigris and Euphrates rivers. Clay tablets dated around 2000 B.C. refer to them, and they were definitely enjoyed by the Assyrians and Babylonians before the time of Jesus. The Chinese are said to have cultivated apricot trees even earlier, more than two thousand years before the Christian era.

The apricot tree (Prunus armeniaca) still bursts into pink splendor so early in the spring that in northern locations a late frost may destroy it. (By planting trees where their buds may be retarded — on a northern slope or northern side of a building or shaded by tall trees to the east — a crop can sometimes be coaxed to survive.)

The fruit, used for dessert, canning, drying, and preserving, can generally be grown anywhere peaches thrive. A ripe, golden apricot just touched with a faint blush bears little resemblance to fruit that has been picked green and shipped for long distances. If you are lucky enough to grow your own, it pays not to be in a hurry. Leaving apricots on the tree as long as possible allows the fruit to reach a state of luscious temptation.

Richest in vitamin A, apricots are also high in potassium, one of the elements known to nourish the heart. Its iron and other minerals are beneficial to people with anemia, tuberculosis, asthma, bronchitis, or blood impurities. High in natural sugars, apricots are fairly low in calories. Three medium fresh apricots total only fifty-five.

The trees went forth on a time to anoint a king over them; and they said unto the olive tree, Reign thou over us. But the olive tree said unto them, Should I leave my fatness, wherewith by me they honour God and man, and go to be promoted over the trees? And the trees said to the fig tree, Come thou, and reign over us. But the fig tree said unto them, Should I forsake my sweetness, and my good fruit, and go to be promoted over the trees? Then said the trees

 *unto the vine, Come thou, and reign over us. And the vine said unto them, Should I leave my wine, which cheereth God and man, and go to be promoted over the trees? Then said all the trees unto the bramble, Come thou, and reign over us. And the bramble said unto the trees, If in truth ye anoint me king over you, then come and put your trust in my shadow: and if not, let fire come out of the bramble, and devour the cedars of Lebanon.*

(Judges 9:8-15)

Bramble fruit (Rubus ulmifolius) includes blackberries, raspberries, dewberries, and loganberries, but blackberries are the ones known to Bible people. They belong to the rose family, a very prickly group.

For every tree is known by his own fruit. For of thorns men do not gather figs, nor of a bramble bush gather they grapes.

(Luke 6:44)

Each berry is actually a bunch of small fruits called drupelets. Black-berries are propagated by suckers and root cuttings. Red flowers are fol-lowed by red fruit which ripens to purple-black. Once again homegrown fruit is superior to that picked for market — too often hard, green, acid, and lacking in flavor. The best ripe berries drop into the warmth of the hand at the gentlest touch.

Considered a good blood cleanser, blackberries are recommended for constipation, anemia, obesity, weak kidneys, rheumatism, arthritis, gout, and skin problems. They're not bad with cream, either.

Getting back to the what-kind-of-fruit-did-Eve-bite-into flap, scholars mention citron (Citrus medica). This refers to a large, lemon-like tender citrus fruit (whose thick peel is candied for use in cakes and confectionery) and whose history is not easy to trace. A few Sanskrit words refer to vari-eties of citron including a sweet one, known in Mesopotamia and Persia where the Greeks encountered it and named it the Persian apple.

The early Hebrews used citron in religious festivals and called it goodly fruit as a way of thanking the Lord for its sweet bounty.

> *Also in the fifteenth day of the seventh month, when ye*
> *have gathered in the fruit of the land, ye shall keep a*
> *feast unto the Lord seven days: on the first day shall be a*
> *sabbath, and on the eighth day shall be a sabbath. And ye*
> *shall take you on the first day the boughs of goodly trees,*
> *branches of palm trees, and the boughs of thick trees, and*
> *willows of the brook; and ye shall rejoice before the Lord*
> *your God seven days.*
>
> (Leviticus 23:39-40)

Just in case you think the reference to the goodly trees is too general
and could apply to any worthy or beneficent fruit bearer, Josephus, the Hebrew historian of the first century A.D. reports that it was a particular tree
on whose boughs grew the citron.

It grows about ten feet high, with a gray-white bark and thick branches.
So far, it sounds like an orange or lemon tree. Its evergreen leaves and
blossoms could be mistaken for them, too, five white and purple petals
(does anybody know why so many flower petals come in fives?) around a
gold center. But the citron fruit is as large as a cucumber, elongated like
some kinds of melons, with a rough, bright yellow bumpy skin and a pleasant smell. Like the lemon, its juice is sour.

Maybe the reason this is thought by some to be the original forbidden
fruit that Eve couldn't resist is due to the indentations on the skin. Someone decided they resembled tooth marks and suggested they could have
been made by the First Mother. Someone else figured they were put there
by the First Father and so they were sometimes called Adam's Apples.

The Hebrew *etz hadar* or goodly trees has been verified by scholars as
Citrus medica possibly introduced from India into the Near East at a very
early date and grown in the Holy Land at the time of the Bible.

We're going to go with their conclusion and use citrus fruits in our
recipes since our elders did utilize them, and besides, we've never seen
fresh citrons in any market in this country. They are grown in Israel and ex-
ported to Jews throughout the world to celebrate Sukkoth.

> *The righteous shall flourish like the palm tree: he shall*
> *grow like a cedar in Lebanon. Those that be planted in*
> *the house of the Lord shall flourish in the courts of our*
> *God. They shall still bring forth fruit in old age; they*
> *shall be fat and flourishing . . .*
>
> (Psalms 92:12-14)

The date palm (Phoenix dactylifera) is one of the Holy Land's most venerable fruit trees. Date palms existed in prehistoric times. The modern botanical name refers to a belief that if burned to the ground, it springs up out of the ashes like the mythical bird.

In Assyrian and Babylonian lands, dates formed the mainstay of the inhabitants' diets for over seven thousand years. It was the Assyrians' food, wine, and honey. Dates were eaten fresh, dried, or pressed into cakes. In the Old Testament, Jericho is called the city of palm trees. Large plantations provided sugar, food, and wine. Palm leaves became a symbol of victory after Theseus broke branches from the date palm to celebrate his victory over the Minotaur. Another tale is that Mary gave birth to Jesus under a palm tree and so any woman who has just given birth should eat three dates.

When fully grown, the date palm can reach a hundred feet in the air. Six foot long compound leaves are arranged like a crown on top of a single trunk. The dates hang in clusters below the leaves. Male and female flowers are borne on different trees and while dates can develop from unpollinated flowers, the fruit from such trees is inferior and seedless. To assist pollination, the grower ties branches of male flower clusters among the female flower clusters at the correct time. Propagation is by suckers, which develop at the base of and reach as high as ten feet up the trunk.

The Babylonians knew how to fertilize the date palm. An ancient bas-relief shows an angel pollinating a female tree with male blossoms. Because of the date palm's sexuality, the ancient Hindus believed it was just one step removed from the animal kingdom and endowed with intelligence.

Dates, a concentrated carbohydrate approximately 75 percent sugar, are an excellent substitute for candy, a good source of calcium, and supply small amounts of minerals and the B vitamins. Fresh dates are moist and plump with a smooth glossy skin. They should be refrigerated in sealed containers.

Date sugar, available in natural food stores, can be substituted for granulated white and brown sugars in recipes. Use in the same proportions as white sugar.

For, lo, the winter is past, the rain is over and gone; The flowers appear on the earth; the time of the singing of birds is come, and the voice of the turtle is heard in our land; The fig tree putteth forth her green figs, and the vines with the tender grape give a good smell. Arise, my love, my fair one, and come away.

(Song of Solomon 2:11-13)

The original fruit named in the Bible (Ficus carica) is known for its leaves used to cover the First Couple in the Garden of Eden.

> *And the eyes of them both were opened, and they knew that they were naked; and they sewed fig leaves together, and made themselves aprons.*

(Genesis 3:7)

The large, rough leaves of the fig tree fall at the beginning of winter and unfold in early spring. The milky gum in all parts of the tree is a skin irritant. What we think of as the fruit of the small fig tree is actually the swollen, hollow receptacle with a small opening in the end opposite the stem, completely lined with tiny flowers, which develop into the true fruits — the fig seeds — after a tiny fig wasp enters and fertilizes the blossoms.

Whether eaten fresh, canned, or dried, and threaded on long strings, figs have a delectable flavor. Dried figs contain over 55 percent natural fruit sugar plus large amounts of iron, vitamin B$_1$, and calcium.

Depending on the variety, the skin can range from pale yellow through bright green to purple-black and their fleshy insides from pale pink to deep scarlet. For really ripe fruit — the best kind — look for slightly wrinkled figs just starting to split at the bottom. They bruise easily and are very perishable. Avoid figs with spotted skins, which indicates that the fruit has turned sour.

It has been said that figs help to relieve low blood pressure, anemia, colitis, gout, skin diseases, and constipation.

The ancients did not lack for sweeteners.

> *Behold, the days come, saith the Lord, that the plowman shall overtake the reaper, and the treader of grapes him that soweth seed; and the mountains shall drop sweet wine, and all the hills shall melt.*

(Amos 9:13)

One of mankind's oldest fruits, fifteen hundred varieties of grape (Vitis vinifera) have been cultivated since prehistoric times and have formed a cornucopia spilling forth an endless supply of food and drink: fresh fruit and juice; dried raisins; grape leaves for cooking; wine; vinegar; and a sweet syrup when the fresh juice was boiled down to the consistency of molasses.

The Hittites cultivated grapes extensively, and the earliest tomb paintings show vines well-established in Egypt. Remains of grapes have been found in funerary offerings. At Lachish, a city in the Holy Land, archaeological finds dated around the beginning of the Bronze Age provide evidence of the use of raisins.

When Noah left the ark and stepped onto dry land, he planted a vineyard. The vines (then, as well as now) are trained to droop their pale creamy yellow, light green, ruby red, or deep, rich purple fruit over porches, pergolas, fence posts, trellises, arbors, and summerhouses. When not supported, they trail along the ground.

The vine is a climbing shrub from whose base numerous slender branches sprout, ascending by means of long tendrils that entwine. The leaves are divided into five-toothed lobes, unfolding in early spring. By late summer, they drop off. Bees pollinate the tiny green flowers. The fruit is a berry containing two seeds in each of its two cells.

Ancient harvesters began by cutting the bunches with a sickle in July and continuing through October. The grapes were thrown into a winepress, then trodden underfoot by laborers. The vintage season was a time of rejoicing, of celebration when the wine was mixed with water and drunk with joy. The vine was and still remains a powerful symbol of prosperity and God's blessing.

> *And they came unto the brook of Eshcol, and cut down from thence a branch with one cluster of grapes, and they bare it between two upon a staff; and they brought of the pomegranates, and of the figs.*
> (Numbers 13:23)

Grapes are a source of quick energy. An alkaline fruit, they help decrease the acidity of uric acid and work to normalize the entire system.

If grown at home, let grapes ripen on the vine to develop maximum sugar concentration. To prolong freshness, cut off the vine with a portion of the main stem. Insert stem end in a jar of water.

Does it surprise you that watermelons were eaten by Bible people?

> *We remember the fish, which we did eat in Egypt freely; the cucumbers, and the melons . . .*
> (Numbers 11:5)

Watermelons have been grown along the banks of the Nile since the Bronze Age. A trailing vine member of the cucurbit family (Citrullus vulgaris) with large globular green, mottled, or striped fruits, it yields red flesh — a luscious and refreshing midsummer joy on a hot day.

But one that sparked another controversy. Some authorities say the correct meaning of the Hebrew word usually translated as "cucumber" is really "muskmelons" and, therefore, cucumbers did not grow in Biblical times, but melons did. Other Biblical botanists point out that since the text says both cucumbers and melons, they must have had both. We lean toward the latter explanation since both were cultivated for thousands of years in Egypt, and Sumerian records from 2000 B.C. mention melons.

All cantaloupes are muskmelons, but not all muskmelons are cantaloupes. Other muskmelons are casaba, honeydew, and Persian.

The word "musk" is Persian for a kind of perfume. A ripe cantaloupe has a definite fragrance at the stem end, the netting is raised, coarse, and dry. A cantaloupe has almost one hundred times more vitamin A than casabas or honeydews.

This is another fruit which is best left on the vine until thoroughly ripe, when it makes a characteristic muffled, dull, thudding sound as it is thumped with the index finger, and the rind closest to the ground has turned from white to pale yellow.

The ancients used it for drink and medicine as well as food. In a hot climate, there's nothing like it — except maybe a pomegranate.

The pomegranate tree (Punica granatum) has been grown since prehistoric times and was once more highly thought of than it is today.

> *And Saul tarried in the uttermost part of Gibeah under a pomegranate tree which is in Migron: and the people that were with him were about six hundred men . . .*
>
> (I Samuel 14:2)

The pomegranate is a large shrub or small tree known for its brilliant orange-red flowers and large red, hard-rinded, juicy, pulpy fruit with many seeds. A ripe pomegranate is about the size of an orange.

> *Thy lips are like a thread of scarlet, and thy speech is comely: thy temples are like a piece of a pomegranate within thy locks.*
>
> (Song of Solomon 4:3)

An old legend claims that the tree of life in the Garden of Eden was the pomegranate.

In Egypt the pomegranate was sacred. The flowers were used as the basis for the design of Solomon's crown. That same design became the model for crowns down through the ages.

Pomegranate trees are long-lived, with surviving specimens over two hundred years old.

In one of the earliest of the Homeric tales, when Persephone was carried away by Pluto to the underworld, her mother, the goddess Demeter, obtained her release on condition that she eat nothing in the underworld. Persephone could not resist the pomegranate. She ate six seeds. Because she did, she could only spend six months above ground. The rest of the time she had to make do with gray and doleful winter, all because of six pomegranate seeds.

The fruit's many seeds epitomize fertility. Seeds always do, but in this case the seeds and the fertility tied in with Persephone.

Parts of the pomegranate were once used medicinally. Maybe because they're high in potassium. The bark and rind were ground into ink and are still used today for tanning leather. The seeds are eaten fresh, dried, and sprinkled on foods or as a confection. Grenadine is a syrup made from the juice.

> *I would lead thee, and bring thee into my mother's house, who would instruct me: I would cause thee to drink of spiced wine of the juice of my pomegranate.*
>
> (Song of Solomon 8:2)

To extract the juice, first roll the fruit back and forth on a counter, pressing against it the way you knead a lemon. Once you cut it open, you can use a citrus reamer, then strain the juice. You can also twist the seeds inside a heavy cheesecloth or experiment with an electric juicer, the kind you feed fruits into, not a citrus juicer. Another possibility is to halve the pomegranates and scoop the seeds into a blender or food processor. Blend very briefly, then press through a strainer.

Pomegranate juice stains, but can be removed with lemon juice. The simplest way to eat a pomegranate is to cut one in half, peel off the bitter membrane, and spoon out the juicy seeds. Either spit out the seeds after chewing or, if you have a mouthful of perfect teeth, crunch the seeds.

> *I went down into the garden of nuts to see the fruits of the valley, and to see whether the vine flourished, and the pomegranates budded.*
>
> (Song of Solomon 6:11)

The Hebrew word "*egoz*" means walnut. Recent translators agree that the above should be translated: "Down I went to the walnut bower to see the green plants of the Bible." How about "orchard" for "bower?"

In ancient times, walnuts (Juglans regia) grew wild in Persia, Greece, Asia Minor, Kashmir, Nepal, and the Orient. The best came from Persia. Josephus, the venerated Hebrew historian, writes of very old walnut trees growing in Palestine.

Roman tradition links the walnut to Jupiter and Juno and walnuts, another fertility symbol, became a feature of wedding ceremonies and feasts.

Pliny gave walnuts credit for magical healing, It is said that chewing a walnut while fasting is a sovereign remedy against the bite of a mad dog.

Deciduous and clean branched with strong trunks, walnut trees swing their graceful foliage close to the ground, providing welcome shade in hot climates. The Persian walnut's bark is silvery gray and smooth, its leaves fragrant. The small green flowers appear before the leaves unfold. The male flowers grow in long catkins and the female in clusters. The wind pollinates them and the round fruits ripen at the end of summer. The outer husk cracks open while still on the tree and allows the thin-shelled, tan nuts to fall to the ground.

Walnuts have a high proportion of unsaturated fatty acids. They build muscles, strong healthy teeth and gums, improve metabolism, and help to correct liver ailments.

> *He heweth him down cedars, and taketh the cypress and the oak, which he strengtheneth for himself among the trees of the forest: he planteth an ash, and the rain doth nourish it.*
>
> (Isaiah 44:14)

In the original language, the cypress in the above passage was "*tirzah*" which led the translator into Arabic to render it as "stone pine," a handsome, parasol-shaped tree with gray-brown bark. The cones are shiny brown.

Whether it was a pine, a cedar or a cypress, pine nuts (Pinus pinea) have been harvested since prehistoric times. Pignoli were relished in ancient Rome and still are enjoyed, although they've become a luxury item because of the difficulty of extracting the nuts from the pine cones.

> *And their father Israel said unto them, If it must be so now, do this; take of the best fruits in the land in your vessels, and carry down the man a present, a little balm, and a little honey, spices, and myrrh, nuts and almonds . . .*
>
> (Genesis 43:11)

There is one other nut tree mentioned in the Good Book.

Pistachios (Pistacia vera) originated in Syria and Persia. A reference in the Talmud makes it clear that the tree has grown in the Holy Land for at least five thousand years.

The trees are deciduous or semi-evergreen with divided leaves. The female trees, broad and bushy, up to thirty feet high, bear fruit after several years if male trees are nearby. The pistachio fruit is reddish and wrinkled. The hard, double-shelled oval nut is inside. They are naturally white but are sometimes sold covered with a red, blue, or green dye.

They are used to flavor ice cream, halvah, and Turkish delight.

The following recipes are for fruit only, fruit in its more natural state, fruit and nuts combined into salads, or primarily fruit desserts. Other fruit (and nut) recipes, mostly those that form the major ingredient in bread, dairy, and desserts will be found at the end of the bread, dairy, and dessert chapters.

JUDEAN FRUIT SALAD

1   cantaloupe
1   honeydew melon
2   baskets blackberries
2   oranges, peeled and wedged
¼   watermelon, cubed
1   lb. seedless grapes, green or red
2   peaches, cubed
    juice of ½ lemon
1   cup yogurt mixed with ⅓ C honey
    mint leaves

Stir fruit pieces together by hand. Squeeze juice of lemon over all. Stir in yogurt. Adjust sweetness with more honey if needed. Garnish with fresh mint leaves.

BLANCHING ALMONDS

To blanch (remove the almond skin), pour boiling water over the nuts, soak ten minutes, and pour off the water. Slip off the skins. Pat dry with paper towels.

A DATE WITH MELONS

2 ripe cantaloupes
½ cup pitted and chopped dates
½ cup raisins
½ cup chopped toasted pistachio nuts
1 cup plain yogurt
2 tbsp. honey

Peel the cantaloupes. Slice into 1-inch thick rings and place on dessert plates. Combine dates, raisins, and nuts. Fill the center of each ring with date-nut mixture. Top with a scoop of yogurt and drizzle honey over the top of each dessert.

BIBLICAL MEDLEY

Mix together ripe Biblical fruits cut into bite-sized pieces. Add raisins. Drizzle a little honey over the top, then sprinkle with ground almonds or chopped walnuts. This may be topped with plain yogurt or cottage cheese.

STUFFED APPLES ATHENA

2 tbsp. raisins
2 tbsp. date pieces
2 tbsp. each chopped walnuts, chopped pistachios,
      slivered almonds and pine nuts
2 tsp. ground cinnamon
¼ cup honey
    zest of ½ lemon
    juice of ½ lemon
6 large apples
1 cup water

Preheat oven to 350°.

Mix together first seven ingredients. Cut off ¾ inch slice from top of each apple. Core, then scoop out pulp. Chop pulp and add to first mixture.

Stuff apple shells with pulp mixture. Place apples close together in a baking pan. Pour the water in the pan, then cover pan tightly with aluminum foil. Bake until apples are tender (about 55 minutes). Uncover. Baste with the syrup in the bottom of the pan. Cool before serving.

APPLE BLACKBERRY SAUL

2 lbs. tart apples, peeled, cored, and sliced
3 tbsp. lemon juice
2 tbsp. honey
½ cup unbleached flour
½ cup date sugar
½ stick butter, cut into small pieces
1 tsp. cinnamon
1 cup fresh blackberries
¾ cup chopped walnuts

Preheat the oven to 375°.

In a large bowl toss the apples with lemon juice and honey. Set aside.

Mix flour, date sugar, butter, and cinnamon. Work the butter into it with your fingers until the mixture is finely crumbled.

Add the blackberries to the apples and turn into a buttered nine or ten inch baking dish. Scatter the chopped walnuts over the top, then add the flour-sugar mixture on top. Bake until the top is golden and crisp, about 35 minutes. Serve warm with cream.

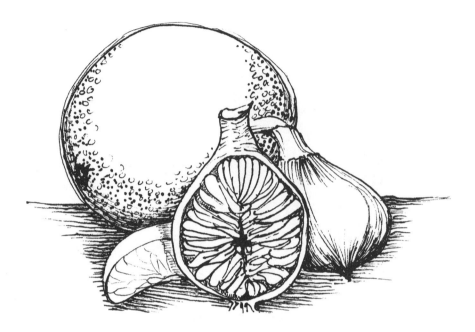

BAKED FIGS IN WINE

15 fresh figs
 2 tsp. orange zest
½ cup orange juice
½ cup rosé or other light wine
 3 tbsp. honey

Preheat the oven to 350°.

Cut the stem ends off the figs. Slice across in half. Set in a shallow baking dish in one layer. Mix together the remaining ingredients and pour over the figs.

Bake until tender, about 20 minutes. Spoon the syrup over each serving.

Chapter Ten

DESSERTS

And I am come down to deliver them out of the hand of the Egyptians, and to bring them up out of that land unto a good land and a large, unto a land flowing with milk and honey . . .

(Exodus 3:8)

Never mind the brave soul who first tried an oyster, what about the first person who figured out how to steal a honeycomb from a swarm of angry bees and put the honey in her mouth? Long life to her in this world and the next!

For the nectar of flowers was transformed into another miracle by the ancients and provided food, medicine, and an alcoholic drink called mead. It was the First Sweetener and, for a long time, the only one.

The Egyptians used honey in their embalming procedures; in India and other eastern countries honey was valued as a method to preserve fruit and, of course, everybody used it to sweeten their lives.

It was thought to have magical properties and conferred health, luck, vitality, and eloquence along with wisdom, purity, and love. Honey has slight antiseptic qualities and has been used to treat wounds, cuts, bruises, and burns. Externally, it relieves skin inflammation. Internally, it soothes intestinal disorders. Including the desire for something sweet.

In those days came John the Baptist, preaching in the wilderness of Judaea. And the same John had his raiment of camel's hair, and a leathern girdle about his loins: and his meat was locusts and wild honey.

(Matthew 3:1,4)

The carob (Ceratonia siliqua) also called the locust or St. John's bread from the earliest days of antiquity because St. John is supposed to have lived on the carob pod while meditating in the desert, is a handsome evergreen tree climbing 50 feet or more. It is native to the eastern Mediterranean area.

Its large pods, rich in protein, are greedily eaten by all kinds of livestock. When people grind them into flour, they yield a powder similar to chocolate but without the theobromine effects (which act like caffeine); the oxalic acid that makes calcium unavailable to the body; the bitterness, which calls for sweetening with sugar; or the high fat content of chocolate. But to be absolutely fair, we've never heard of anyone becoming a carobholic.

Carob is rich in natural sugars and contains pectin which makes it beneficial to treat stomach disorders and diarrhea. It is also rich in vitamins A and B complex.

DINAH'S HONEY CAKE

½ cup almond oil or melted butter
1 cup honey
5 eggs, separated
4 cups whole wheat pastry flour
2 tsp. cinnamon
¼ tsp. salt
½ cup milk

Preheat oven to 350°.

Oil a 9-inch loaf pan. Cream oil and honey. Add well-beaten egg yolks. Sift dry ingredients. Add to mixture, stirring with milk. Beat egg whites until stiff. Carefully fold into mixture. Pour batter into the pan, smoothing top with a spatula. Bake 45 minutes or until cake tester comes out clean.

When cool, ice with:

HONEY ALMOND FROSTING

½ cup honey
1   tsp. almond extract
5   tbsp. flour
    grated rind of 1 orange
4   tsp. orange juice
3   egg yolks
½   cup chopped toasted almonds

Mix together honey, almond extract, and flour. Stir in the juice and the grated orange rind. Whip egg yolks until frothy and whisk into the other mixture. Cook over low heat about ten minutes or until thick and smooth, stirring constantly. Cool. Mix in the toasted almonds, then spread on top of the honey loaf.

SARA'S SPONGE CAKE

  5   eggs, room temperature and separated
  ½ cup cold water
  ¾ cup honey
  ¼ tsp. salt
  4   drops anise extract
  1   cup pastry, all purpose, or cake flour, but not self-rising flour

Preheat the oven to 325°.

Line a 9-inch tube pan with waxed paper that has been cut to fit.

Beat the egg yolks, adding the cold water a little at a time. Beat in half the honey gradually and continue to beat until the mixture peaks for a moment before dropping off a spoon.

In a separate bowl, beat egg whites and when foamy, add salt, anise extract, and the rest of the honey. Continue beating until stiff. Stir a little of the beaten egg whites into the first mixture. Now add the rest of the whites and sift the flour over the top of the bowl before gently folding into the mixture. Spoon into the lined tube pan and bake 45-55 minutes. Check with a cake tester, toothpick, or straw. If it comes out clean, it's done.

Invert to cool completely before removing from the pan. May be served topped with fruit or berries, and/or whipped cream.

MARTHA'S CAROB DATE NUT LOAF

½ cup butter
1 cup honey
½ cup carob powder
4 eggs, separated
1 lb. pitted dates, coarsely chopped
1 lb. chopped walnuts
½ tsp. salt
1 cup whole wheat flour
1 tbsp. grated orange peel

Heat oven to 350°.

Cream butter, honey, and carob in large bowl. Add beaten egg yolks, dates, and nuts. Mix well. Sift in flour and salt, mixing thoroughly. Add grated orange peel. If too dry, add a tablespoon or two of water and mix again. Fold in the stiffly beaten egg whites. Bake in oiled and waxed paper-lined loaf pan for one hour.

STAFF OF LIFE PUDDING

¾-1 stick softened unsalted butter
1¼ cups milk
1¼ cups cream
 1 tsp. orange zest
 3 large eggs
 ½ cup honey
 ¼ tsp. salt
 6 slices white, firm textured bread
   (Italian, French, or homemade)
 ½ cup raisins
 2 tbsp. orange marmalade

Preheat oven to 325°.

Butter a deep 2½ quart casserole. In a heavy-bottomed saucepan, combine milk, cream, and orange zest. Slowly bring to a near boil over low heat. Remove from heat just before it boils. In large mixing bowl, beat together eggs, honey, and salt. Slowly add milk and cream mixture, stirring constantly.

Butter bread with half the butter and arrange on the bottom of the casserole. Sprinkle with raisins, then pour the milk and egg mixture through a strainer over the bread. It doesn't matter if some floats. Dot with the remaining butter and let stand ten minutes.

Cover and bake for 30 minutes, then uncover and bake another 30 minutes. It should be firmly set around the sides. Remove from the oven and lightly spread orange marmalade over the top. Serve warm.

NEHEMIAH'S NUTTY COOKIES

⅓ cup almonds, ground
⅓ cup black walnuts, ground
⅓ cup pine nuts
1 cup pistachio nuts, ground
½ lb. unsalted butter, room temperature
1 cup honey
¾ cup orange juice
¼ tsp. salt
1¾ cups all-purpose flour

These are really best if made a day ahead.

On the first day, measure and grind almonds, walnuts, and pine nuts. Set aside. Grind pistachio nuts separately and set aside.

Place butter in a mixing bowl. Beat with electric mixer.

Gradually add honey while continuing to beat; stir in orange juice and salt. Add ground nuts and flour, except for pistachio nuts; cover with plastic wrap and chill overnight for best results.

The next day preheat oven to 325°.

Break off pieces of dough and roll between palms of your hands to form balls the size of a small walnut. Dip in ground pistachio nuts. Place on ungreased cookie sheets. Return rest of batter to refrigerator between batches.

Bake for 20 minutes. Yield: about 5 dozen.

The cookies are soft when they come out of the oven, but harden as they cool.

LEMON-BLACKBERRY PARFAIT

      grated zest of 2 large lemons
      juice of the 2 lemons, strained
¼ lb. butter
¾ cup honey
4 eggs
2 pints fresh blackberries, washed and drained
2 cups whipped cream
      honey
      fresh mint sprigs for garnish

Cook the lemon zest, juice, butter, and honey in the top of a double boiler, being careful not to let the water boil. Stir occasionally until the butter melts and the honey liquefies.

In a mixing bowl, beat the eggs until blended. Stirring constantly, spoon a bit of the hot lemon mixture into the eggs. Add the egg mixture to the lemon mix, stirring continually until it thickens, about 20 minutes. Remove from the heat. Cool, then refrigerate.

An hour before dinner, assemble as follows. Apportion the blackberries into six parfait glasses. Spoon alternate layers of lemon mixture and whipped cream into the parfait glasses. Drizzle with honey. Garnish with a sprig of mint. Return to refrigerator.

CLEO'S CUSTARD

    3 egg yolks
    1 egg
    ¼ cup honey
    1 cup heavy cream
    1 cup milk
    ½ tsp. lemon zest
       cinnamon

Preheat oven to 325°.

Beat egg yolks and whole egg together until light. Beat in honey. Combine cream and milk, scald, and beat gradually into egg mixture. Stir in lemon zest.

Pour into six individual custard cups. Sprinkle with cinnamon. Place in baking pan and add hot water to reach halfway up sides of cups. Bake for one hour or until a knife inserted into custard comes out clean. Serve hot, warm, or cold.

HANNAH'S CREAM

  8 oz. yogurt pot cheese (made by draining yogurt
       in cheesecloth-lined colander overnight in refrigerator)
  8 oz. cottage cheese
  ⅓ cup honey
  1 cup heavy cream, whipped
  1 pint fresh blackberries

Beat cheeses together until smooth. Gradually add honey and fold in the whipped cream.

Pour into a sieve lined with cheesecloth, set on top of a bowl to drain and refrigerate 12 hours. Turn out onto a platter and serve with fresh blackberries.

RUGELACH

½ lb. unsalted butter
8 oz. cream cheese
2 cups all-purpose flour
½ cup honey
½ cup raisins
1 tsp. cinnamon
1 cup finely chopped nuts
¼ cup orange juice
¼ cup honey

Cream the butter and cream cheese in a food processor. Gradually add the flour, kneading the dough until all the flour is mixed in. Refrigerate at least one hour.

Divide the dough in half.

Combine honey, raisins, cinnamon, chopped nuts and orange juice and set aside.

Preheat oven to 325°.

Lightly flour a board. Roll out one-half of the dough into a circle as thin as possible. With a knife or pastry wheel, cut into 16 wedges. Spread a bit of the filling on each wedge. Beginning at the wide end (the base of the triangle), roll up toward the point. Place on an ungreased cookie sheet you've first covered with foil or be prepared to trash your cookie sheet after the first batch. When the cookie sheet is full, carefully brush the top of each cookie with the rest of the honey.

Bake 20 minutes or until golden brown.

ALMOND BUNS ABSALOM

2   tbsp. yeast
1¾ cups milk, warmed to body temperature
¾   cup almonds, ground
1   cup cottage cheese
3   cups warm milk
¼   cup butter
⅔   cup honey
3¾ cups unbleached pastry flour

Put yeast into 1¾ cups warm milk. Let sit five minutes. Grind almonds in the blender, set aside. Cream cottage cheese and milk in the blender. In a large bowl, cream butter, honey, and flour. Make a well in the center and stir in the cottage cheese mixture, ground almonds, and yeast mixture.

Knead the dough on a floured surface five minutes. Place dough in lightly oiled bowl. Let rise for 45 minutes in a warm place.

Preheat oven to 400°.

Punch down dough and knead again four or five minutes. Roll dough until it is ½ inch thick. Cut in 5-inch rounds. Place buns on lightly oiled cookie sheet. Bake 8-10 minutes. Serve warm. Makes 24 buns.

GOLDEN APRICOTS

¾ cup dried apricots
1 cup water
½ cup butter
½ cup honey
1⅓ cups pastry flour
2 large eggs
½ cup plain yogurt
1 tsp. orange zest
½ cup honey

Butter an 8-inch square baking dish. Place apricots and 1 cup water in a saucepan. Bring to a boil, reduce heat, and simmer 10-15 minutes until apricots are tender. Drain and let cool.

Preheat oven to 350°.

Using a food processor, combine butter, ½ cup honey, and 1 cup flour. Process until smooth. Spread evenly in a prepared baking dish. Bake 15 minutes.

In food processor, chop drained apricots into ¼-inch pieces. Add ⅓ cup flour, eggs, yogurt, orange zest, and the other ½ cup of honey. Process until mixed well, about 6–8 seconds.

Remove crust from oven, spread apricot mixture evenly over baked crust and return to oven for another 25 minutes.

Let cool, then cut into 2-inch squares.

For a rich, delicious dessert, spread honey almond frosting between the layers and whipped cream on top.

JACOB AND ESAU — WHAT A PEAR

2   sticks cinnamon
    piece of lemon rind
½   cup red wine
¾   cup honey
6   pears
1   pt. whipping cream
¼   tsp. peppermint extract

Add cinnamon and lemon rind to wine and honey in a large kettle. Bring just to boiling, turn heat to low, and simmer 5-10 minutes.

Peel, core, and halve pears and place in simmering wine mixture. Simmer 10 minutes, remove from heat. Allow pears to steep in wine mixture at least 20 minutes. Remove pears to serving dish. Discard lemon rind and cinnamon. Cook syrup until reduced to half its original quantity. Pour over pears. May be served warm or chilled.

For a company dinner, you may want to whip 1 pint of chilled whipping cream with the peppermint extract until very stiff. Heap whipped cream in between two pear halves so it acts as a kind of mortar holding the halves when they are pressed together, with just a bit of cream showing at the edges.

LUKE'S LEMON CUSTARD

3 tbsp. butter
1 cup lemon juice
1 cup honey
1½ cups milk
½ cup whole wheat pastry flour
3 eggs, beaten
2 tsp. lemon zest
1 pt. whipping cream
¼ cup honey
¾ cup ground almonds

Melt the butter in a saucepan. Add the lemon juice, honey, milk, and flour, and cook over medium heat until the mixture begins to boil.

Remove from heat and add the beaten eggs and lemon zest. Cook another 5 minutes, stirring constantly, and then pour into dessert cups. Chill for at least 2 hours.

Just before serving, add honey to the whipped cream. Spoon whipped cream over pudding. Sprinkle with ground almonds.

MOUSSE MENANDER

2 cups whipping cream
½ cup carob powder
¼ cup honey
6 lightly beaten egg yolks
¼ tsp. peppermint flavoring

Combine cream, carob, and honey and cook over very low heat, stirring constantly until blended and the cream is scalded. Remove from heat. Beat the egg yolks and the peppermint flavoring into the mixture.

Pour into small (it's very rich) *pot de crème* or custard cups and chill at least 4 hours before serving.

ELDERS' HONEY CAKE WITH BERRIES

½ cup butter
1 cup wildflower honey
½ cup yogurt
½ cup cream
4 tbsp. lemon juice
1½ cups whole wheat pastry flour
½ tsp. salt
¾ tsp. cinnamon
⅔ cup walnuts, chopped
3 pts. blackberries
1 cup apricot sauce (prepare night before, see below)
1 tbsp. mint, chopped

Preheat oven to 350°.

Cream butter and whisk in honey, yogurt, cream, and one tablespoon of the lemon juice. Mix flour, salt, cinnamon, and walnuts. Combine ingredients gently. Do not whip or beat. Butter an 8-inch square pan. Pour batter into pan and bake for 45 minutes until skewer comes out clean. Cool and unmold onto cake rack.

APRICOT SAUCE

Soak ½ lb. dried apricots in 2 cups water overnight. Next day bring to a boil and simmer until soft. Purée in blender or food processor with ¼ cup light honey. Return to heat and simmer until thick.

Combine berries, mint, and remaining lemon juice with apricot sauce. Heap onto cake.

A TO ZION PASTRIES

1⅓ cups whole wheat pastry flour
½ tsp. salt
½ cup butter
4-5 tbsp. water
1 cup apples, sliced thin
1 tbsp. whole wheat pastry flour
½ cup honey
2 tbsp. almonds, sliced
3 tbsp. apricot sauce (see Elders' Honey Cake)

Preheat oven to 450°.

Sift 1⅓ cup flour with the salt into a large mixing bowl. Cut in the butter with pastry blender until mixture is the size of small peas. Sprinkle 4-5 tablespoons water, a little at a time, over the flour while stirring with a fork, until mixture is just moist enough to hold together.

Form into a square and flatten to ½ inch. Roll out on floured surface to 12 inch square. Place on ungreased cookie sheet.

Toss sliced apples with 1 tablespoon of flour. Place slices down center third of dough. Drizzle half the honey over apples. Fold up about ½ inch at each end. Fold sides over apples, leaving an inch of apples showing down center. Sprinkle with the rest of the honey and the sliced almonds.

Bake for 15-20 minutes or until golden brown.

Spread immediately with apricot sauce.

HONEY PUFFS HESTIA

    2   pkgs. dry yeast
    ½   cup warm water
    1   cup warm milk
    4   tbsp. honey
    1   tsp. salt
    2   eggs, lightly beaten
    ½   cup butter, melted and cooled
  3-4   cups sifted flour
        olive oil, lightest flavor
    1   cup honey
        ground cinnamon

In a small bowl, sprinkle yeast over the half-cup of warm water and let soften about 5 minutes.

Meanwhile, pour milk into a large bowl and add the 2 tablespoons of honey and salt. Stir in the yeast mixture and eggs; add butter and beat well. Slowly add 3 cups of flour, beating continuously until the batter is smooth. Add more flour as needed, but don't expect it to look like a stiff bread dough. It should be soft. Cover bowl with a towel and let dough rise in a warm place 2 to 3 hours until doubled in bulk.

In a medium saucepan, pour oil to a depth of 3 or 4 inches and heat to a frying temperature (360°). While the oil is heating, pour about a cup of honey into a small saucepan and warm over very low heat.

Stir batter. Drop batter from a tablespoon into the hot oil. Turn when it forms puffs. Let them become golden brown on all sides. Drain on paper towels, then arrange a layer on a platter, drizzle with warm honey and dust with cinnamon. Top with a second layer of puffs. Continue until all are layered. Serve.

Makes about 3 dozen puffs.

Chapter Eleven

FESTIVE MENUS

Here are some menus for entertaining Bible style, dinners built around a chicken, fish, or a vegetarian main course, all strictly adhering to the premise that we can eat what *they* ate while preparing it *our* way. These are only suggestions meant to encourage you to use the principles outlined in this book to create your own menus.

Each recipe serves six but may be cautiously expanded to feed a larger crowd, keeping in mind that simply multiplying measurements sometimes produces quixotic results.

Each menu may be accompanied by the proper wine; knowing how the ancients revered wine.

Along with the good food and the fine wine we salute you with a heartfelt:

Prosit!
À votre santé!
Gun-bei!
Skål!
Slàinte!
Na zdorovye!
Stinyia ssais!
L'chayim!

Here are recipes for some seasonal festivals celebrated by Jews around the world.

ROSH HASHANAH, the high holy days that begin the Jewish New Year, arrives in autumn, (late September or early October), and commemorates the time God allowed Abraham to substitute a ram for his son, Isaac, as a sacrifice. It is, therefore, symbolic of the faith of Abraham and the Hebrew people. It is also a time of self-examination and repentance.

The dinner table on Rosh Hashanah features harvest foods and dishes representing a sweet future to come in the new year with honey, raisins, prunes, carrots & apples—no sour or bitter dishes; loaves of round challah, fish, and new fruits so that the coming year will be round, smooth and sweet. The new fruits of the season feature apples, persimmons, and pomegranates.

Menu:

Egg Lemon Soup Athenaeus (p. 34)
Fillets of Sole en Vino e Grappe (p. 125)
Methusalah's Egg Bread (p. 134)*
Rich as Croesus' Mint Salad (p. 71)
Carrots and Turnips Zebulun (p. 51)
Stuffed Apples Athena (p. 162)
Dinah's Honey Cake (p. 167)

*Roll dough into rope about 24" long, then coil rope into a spiral creating a round loaf. Continue with original recipe.

YOM KIPPUR, the Day of Atonement, is the most solemn day of the Jewish year, observed by prayer, self-examination, and fasting. On Yom Kippur Eve the meal before the next day's fasting might feature chicken, carrots, fresh fruit (no nuts), and end with a symbolic bit of bread and water to signify that one will be sustained throughout the fast.

Menu:

Mrs. Noah's Chicken (p. 114)
Sweet Anise Challah (p. 137)
Carrot Rolls (p. 50)
Green Salad with Salad Dressing Hosea (p. 66)
Fresh Fruit

SUKKOTH is a Jewish harvest festival. It commemorates the time when the Jews lived in the desert in huts and tents after their exodus from Egypt. It is also known as the Feast of the Ingathering:

> *. . . and the feast of ingathering, which is in the end of the year, when thou hast gathered in thy labours out of the field.*
>
> (Exodus 23:16)

It is traditional to eat citron if you can find it (or oranges); figs, dates, pomegranates, apricots, grapes, olives, romaine lettuce, onions, barley & wheat bread. Again, the citron is what the ancients in Egypt knew as *etrog*, not the modern orange—hard to come by in this country. We wonder if it doesn't resemble the Seville orange, perfect for making marmalade, but much too bitter to bite into.

Menu:

Aromatic Fennel Soup (p. 29)
Rosemary Loaves (p. 140)
Roamin' Salad (p. 76)
Staff of Life Pudding (p. 171)
or
Baked Figs in Wine (p. 164)

CHANUKAH, the Feast of Lights, commemorates the time the Maccabees recaptured the Jerusalem Temple. The Israelites discovered there was only enough oil for one day, but miraculously the oil to light the temple lasted eight days and nights. Chanukah is a celebration of survival.

It isn't clear where the tradition began, but Eastern European Jews eat some form of *latkes* (pancakes) made with oil; Greeks prepare *loukomades* (deep-fried puffs dipped in honey); Persian Jews make *zelebi*; and in Israel they eat *sufganiyot*, a jam-filled, deep-fried doughnut.

Menu:

Salmon Latkes (p. 130)
Salad Joshua (p. 73)
Honey Puffs Hestia (p. 185)
Rugelach (p. 176)
Mint Tea

PURIM, the last holiday before Passover, celebrates the end of winter, a joyous welcome to spring and a festival celebrating the bravery of Queen Esther, married to a Persian King, who saved her people from slaughter. The word "purim" means "lots" and refers to the casting of lots to determine the day the Jews would die before Queen Esther intervened. It is, therefore, a day usually in February or March celebrating survival and the sharing of goodies between households.

Foods eaten are *kreplach* (a meat- or cheese-filled egg-noodle dough akin to ravioli, wanton, and pirogi), other stuffed pastries, chickpeas, turkey or chicken, and, since this was considered the last opportunity to use up the year's flour before Passover, every variety of baked goods.

Menu:

Chickpea Soup David (p. 32)
Hagar's Honey Chick (p. 124)
Kreplach (p. 115)
Salad with Heaven on Earth Dressing (p. 65)
Golden Apricots (p. 178)

PASSOVER, PESACH,

 Thou shalt keep the feast of unleavened bread: (thou shalt eat unleavened bread seven days, as I commanded thee, in the time appointed of the month Abib; for in it thou camest out from Egypt: and none shall appear before me empty:)

(Exodus 23:15)

Passover was originally a nature festival observed by nomadic desert Jews. Later it evolved into a festival celebrating freedom, the exodus of the Jews from Egypt and God passing over Jewish houses when he slew the firstborn in Egypt. When the Jews fled, they had no time to wait for their bread to rise so Jews around the world eat nothing made with regular flour or leavening agents for this holiday. They use special dishes, cutlery and utensils kept for Passover use beginning with seders on the first two nights. Instead of bread, they eat matzos (no salt or yeast), egg dishes, lamb, wine, apples, nuts, and sponge cake.

Menu:

Honey Walnut Trout (p. 131)
Asparagus Aaron (p. 44)
Matzos
Kidney Bean Salad (p. 76)
Sara's Sponge Cake (p. 169)

The merchandise of gold, and silver, and precious stones, and of pearls, and fine linen, and purple, and silk, and scarlet, and all thy fine wood, and all manner vessels of ivory, and all manner vessels of most precious wood, and of brass, and iron, and marble, And cinnamon, and odours, and ointments, and frankincense, and wine, and oil, and fine flour, and wheat, and beasts, and sheep, and horses, and chariots, and slaves, and souls of men. And the fruits that thy soul lusted after are departed from thee, and all things which were dainty and goodly are departed from thee, and thou shalt find them no more at all.

(Revelation 18:12-14)

Gloom? Or a timely reminder of fleeting days? We leave that to the theologians. As for us, we hope to cherish whatever time we have left. We wish you, most sincerely, the same.

And when we gather at our tables, counting our blessings for bounty and loved ones, we might remember all those who came before, women mostly, who were the traditional cooks before more recent generations — women who blistered their palms over open fires, who broke their backs lugging water across rocky plains, who scalded and stuffed, peeled and pared, who rolled out and patted and mashed and baked, in unlovely farmhouses, cabins, and tenement flats — all the women who fed us, in an unbroken line all the way back to the kitchen of Eve. Remember and give thanks.

Then shall thy light break forth as the morning, and thine health shall spring forth speedily: and thy righteousness shall go before thee; the glory of the Lord shall be thy reward.

(Isaiah 58:8)

Enjoy.

BIBLIOGRAPHY

Bass, Lorena LaForest. *Honey and Spice*. Ashland, Oregon: Coriander Press, 1983.

Brothwell, Don. *Food in Antiquity*. New York: Praeger, 1969.

Davenport, Rita. *Sourdough Cookery*. Tucson, Arizona: Bantam Books, 1977.

Dulin, Rachel. *Old Age in the Hebrew Scriptures,* Ph.D. Dissertation: Northwestern University, 1982.

Edwards, John. *Roman Cookery of Apicius*. Point Roberts, Washington: Hartley and Marks, 1984.

Encyclopaedia Britannica. 1967.

Fiszer, Louise & Ferrary, Jeanette. *Jewish Holiday Feasts*. San Francisco: Chronicle Books, 1995.

Goodman, Naomi, Marcus, Robert, Woolhandler, Susan. *The Good Book Cookbook*. New York: Dodd, Mead and Company, 1986.

Gower, Ralph. *New Manners and Customs of Bible Times*. Chicago: Moody Press, 1987.

Green, Henrietta. *A Glorious Harvest*. New York: Sedgewood Press, 1992.

Kinard, Malvina. *Loaves and Fishes*. New Canaan, Connecticut: Keats, 1975.

King James Version. *The Holy Bible*.

Klein, Isaac. *A Guide to Jewish Religious Practice*. New York: Jewish Theological Seminary of America, 1979.

Kochilas, Diane. *Food and Wine of Greece.* New York: St. Martin's Press, 1990.

Lasalle, George. *George Lasalle's Middle Eastern Food.* London, England: Kyle Cathie Limited, 1991.

Leonard, Jonathan Norton. *The First Farmers.* Time, Inc., 1973.

Lerner, Carol. *A Biblical Garden.* New York: William Morrow and Co., 1982.

Matthews, Victor H. *Manners and Customs in the Bible.* Peabody, Massachusetts: Hendrickson Publishers, 1988.

McKibbin, Jean and Frank. *Cookbook of Foods From Bible Days.* Frank McKibbin, 1972.

McMillen, S.I. M.D. *None of These Diseases.* Old Tappan, New Jersey: Fleming H. Revell Co.,1963, 1984.

Nathan, Joan. *The Jewish Holiday Kitchen.* New York: Schocken Books, 1979.

Shewell-Cooper, W. E. *Plants and Fruits of the Bible.* London: Darton, Longman and Todd, 1962.

Wise Garden Encyclopedia, The. New York: Wm. H. Wise and Co., Inc., 1959.

Walker, Winifred. *All the Plants of the Bible.* Garden City, New York: Doubleday and Co., 1979.

Zohary, Michael. *Plants of the Bible.* London: Cambridge University Press, 1982.

Index